EXPLORATION

◆ The Total Curriculum ◆

D1608930

Mary F. Compton and Horace C. Hawn

NATIONAL MIDDLE SCHOOL ASSOCIATION

NATIONAL MIDDLE SCHOOL ASSOCIATION

Mary F. Compton is Professor of Education Emerita, University of Georgia, Athens. A former president of the National Middle School Association and an early national leader, Dr. Compton continues to work with school systems and institutions of higher education on educational improvement projects.

Horace C. Hawn is Associate Professor of Education Emeritus, also at the University of Georgia. Dr. Hawn now pursues his long standing interest and involvement in middle level education as a consultant.

The National Middle School Association is appreciative of the professional contribution of these authors and is pleased to present this important volume. Gratitude is also expressed to Mary Mitchell for her careful work in preparing the manuscript for printing.

Copyright © 1993 by the National Middle School Association
4807 Evanswood Drive, Columbus, Ohio 43229-6292

ISBN: 56090-067-9

To Bill Alexander—
teacher, mentor, friend

Content Overview

Table of Contents

Foreword

The curriculum has a responsibility to open the mind as much as to fill it. This view of curriculum, which has real validity at the middle level, will be especially well-served by this new volume. *Exploration: The Total Curriculum* raises questions and ideas that will open the mind, present new vistas and intriguing possibilities that will lead pupils in pursuit of new knowledge, and encourage problem-solving.

If you want to make your subject more relevant; if you want to help youngsters understand the world in which they are now living; if you want to stimulate pupils to engage in critical thinking; this publication is for you. It is a reservoir of specifics that will make evident the exploratory possibilities inherent in every subject area. A review of the table of contents will reveal the scope of this volume. The innumerable, but often overlooked, exploratory opportunities that reside in the four basic subject areas are amply illustrated. In the same manner the typical exploratory areas — art, music, etc. — all are treated generously. Throughout its pages, possibilities for integrating the various subject areas are also suggested by the authors.

Beyond the immediate and functional aspects of this book, it has continuing importance because it sets forth a point of view about exploration that has not received the attention it should. Too many still see exploration as a limited responsibility that can be taken care of by way of special courses so labelled. As implied in the title, exploration is inherent in the total middle level curriculum. In fact, it is a distinguishing and unique aspect of middle level education. This is most appropriate since young adolescents are in a stage of development that inevitably calls for exploration. They are adventuresome and curious and are moving into a phase of intellectual maturity that has them asking *Why? How come? Is it true that?* They are ready to consider issues and topics that would not have occurred to them a year or two earlier.

Asking students to cover a totally pre-planned and prescribed curriculum violates the nature of young adolescents and fails to capitalize on the wonderful curiosity that characterizes them. This book will help you exploit more fully these highly desirable traits of young adolescents. Every faculty member individually and every faculty collectively would do well to spend time sampling this volume. It will open eyes, broaden perspectives, and offer a rich variety of activities worth pursuing.

John H. Lounsbury
Publications Editor, NMSA

CHAPTER ONE

Bases for Exploration

I n 1918 the National Education Association's Commission on the Reorganization of Secondary Education, most famous for its statement of the Seven Cardinal Principles, put its stamp on the idea of extending secondary education downward to include grades seven and eight and dividing these secondary grades into two three-year units, junior high and senior high. Beginning in 1909/1910 a number of junior high schools had already been established.

It is quite likely that at least one committee member may have realized that the name "junior high" was a poor choice. A junior version usually carries an expectation that junior will be easily recognized as the offspring of the original. It is also reasonable to expect that "junior" will be the spitting image of "senior." It is reasonable to expect that this would occur with organizational levels as well as with human families. And it is exactly what happened. The junior high school adopted most of the practices as well as some of the accoutrements of the high school — marching bands, cheerleaders, pep clubs, interscholastic sports. In professional literature as well as in professional organizations and governmental agencies, the junior high school has always been categorized with the senior high school as "secondary education."

Gruhn and Douglass (1947), in an effort to legitimize the junior high as a separate and unique level of organization quite different from the senior high school, offered six functions of the junior high. One of the functions, *exploration,* was described as follows:

> To lead pupils to discover and explore their specialized interests, aptitudes, and abilities as a basis for decisions regarding educational opportunities.

> To lead pupils to discover and explore their specialized interests, aptitudes, and abilities as a basis for present and future vocational decisions.

> To stimulate pupils and provide opportunities for them to develop a continually widening range of cultural, social, civic, avocational, and recreational interests. (p. 59)

The other functions were *integration, guidance, differentiation, socialization,* and *articulation.* The elaborations of these functions included many statements that support the concept of exploration as well as help to define a separate and unique level of schooling.

Pressure from the senior high, misconceptions on the part of the public, and the lack of specially-prepared teachers were among factors which prevented the junior high school from fulfilling these purposes and meeting its potential. As Alexander and George (1981) stated, the junior high, instead of providing the bridge between the elementary school and the high school, provided, at best, an additional abrupt change to which youngsters were required to adjust — and at an earlier age! In too many instances, secondary education with all of its characteristics and pressures was moved into what had earlier been considered elementary education.

Gruhn and Douglass' function of *exploration* was largely met, however inadequately, by special short-term courses and electives. For example, the student who had an obvious interest in instrumental music could "elect" band and/or orchestra. Those whose voices had not changed and who could "carry a tune" with some degree of success might elect to focus on choral music. Those who did not qualify for instrumental or choral music were often given one option — general music. Teachers of general music in the traditional junior high school had a difficult and thankless task. They worked with students who had little knowledge of music and who had little interest in learning the material included in the program. Traditionally, content had little relevance to the students' everyday lives. For example, it is highly unlikely that a topic of dinner conversation in the average home might revolve around the etudes, mazurkas and waltzes of Frederic Chopin. Nor would the identification of key signatures in musical compositions likely be part of the evening's entertainment in most homes.

During the 30s and 40s, other choices were available to junior high school students — depending on the student's sex. Girls might choose home economics or art; boys, industrial arts or art. Because many states required girls to take a single course in home economics at some point within grades 9-12, many chose to enroll during grade nine in order to "get it over with." There was no need to enroll in grade seven or eight because they would not meet the requirement. For these girls who avoided home economics the only option during the seventh and eighth grades was art. Boys may have been pressured by their fathers to choose industrial arts. The manufacture of bookends and broom holders spilled over into many other classrooms — much to the chagrin of teachers who were forced to cope with the soft grating noise and the mess made by boys who seemed to sand these items constantly.

NATURE OF THE MIDDLE SCHOOL STUDENT

The middle school student is a special person capable of demonstrating many skills, expressing extreme creativity, feeling extraordinary empathy, yet acting in callous, even cruel, ways towards others. Capable of bravado one moment and fear and intimidation the next, these youngsters are influenced by their peers while they crave the approval of their parents and siblings. They do not fit any category offered by most psychologists. They are ever-changing — at times a child, then an adult or an adolescent.

They are youngsters who are approximately ten to fourteen years of age and likely to be enrolled in grades six through eight. This group is sometimes referred to as "young adolescents." They are neither children nor fully adolescent. Some have experienced their growth spurt and are well on their way to sexual maturation.

No individual is merely the sum of particular characteristics. We are much, much more. By the same token, educators would agree that it is impossible to categorize accurately human beings by use of single or even multiple traits. However, in order to discuss fully the nature of the learner, we propose to look at the young adolescent from the standpoint of the physical, intellectual, emotional, and social changes that *most* students will experience during their years in the middle school. A curriculum that provides appropriate exploratory activities must be based on knowledge of these learners.

Physical Development

Males and females are not born equal. In fact, although a greater number of males are conceived, more female babies are carried to full term. The male fetus appears to be more prone to miscarriage than is the female. By the time of the onset of adolescence the female is about one and a half to two years ahead of her male counterpart — a fact with some relevance for exploratory experiences.

During the time children are in the elementary grades there is no substantial difference in their size, shape, or physique. Of course, there is a wide range of differences among children at any age and at any grade level, but the average male and the average female in grade three appear quite similar. It is easy to mistake one sex for the other when youngsters appear at the door to sell raffle tickets or magazine subscriptions. Their shapes, sizes, hair styles, and clothing might be defined as "unisex."

When the hypothalamus, that part of the brain that controls the secretions of the pituitary gland and its effect on growth, releases its regulatory power, adolescence begins. Physiologists (Frisch, 1974; Snow, 1989; Tanner, 1978) have written that adolescence begins with the growth spurt. "Puberty," a term that refers to the process of sexual maturation is not synonymous with "adolescence." In females the average age for the onset of puberty — the beginning of menstruation, or menarche, is twelve years of age. Adolescence begins approximately one and a half to two years *before* the onset of puberty. With this in mind it seems logical to assume that the average eleven year old girl may either be on the threshold of adolescence or already "through the door." The average boy, who reaches puberty almost two years later than the average female becomes adolescent at twelve or thirteen years of age. A small, childlike boy and a fully adolescent girl may sit side by side in the sixth, seventh, or eighth grades.

During adolescence and puberty the body undergoes many physical changes. These changes are by no means limited to those that relate to primary and secondary sexual characteristics. The long bones of the arms and legs grow rapidly — before muscular development can catch up. This causes a lack of muscular coordination. Boys' shoulders and girls' hips broaden. The heart grows larger but the rate of heartbeat slows, causing the potential for relatively high blood pressure. Basal metabolism fluctuates so quickly that the youngster's energy level, if plotted on a chart, would appear as erratic as the fever notations on a hospital chart of a malaria patient. The adolescent's blood sugar level, which is very high at breakfast time, may drop dramatically by the time of arrival at school making concentration difficult.

Because of the changes occurring in the shape of the eyeball, many adolescents experience nearsightedness, or myopia. Some have trouble seeing information on the chalkboard or viewing various types of instructional material. Faculties of middle schools cannot operate like the mythical gatekeeper, Procrustes, who stretched travellers' bodies on a bed or lopped off those parts that caused the body not to fit the bed. When one looks at the variations in physical development there are many questions that beg to be answered, such as: What kind of furniture is most appropriate to accommodate the variations in the sizes of the students? Should the school be responsible for providing breakfast programs for students? Should students be grouped for physical education by developmental level? By sex? What should be the nature of physical education programs in the middle school? of exploratory programs? How long should each instructional activity last? What's the optimum length of the school day/school year for this age group?

Intellectual Development

Early adolescents also undergo intellectual changes. The Swiss logician, Jean Piaget (1958), proposed that there are four sequential stages of human intellectual development. None of the stages can be skipped, but not every person will experience all of the stages. Although Piaget suggested ages at which one might move from one stage to the next, he probably never intended that these ages be "set in stone" as the times when changes would occur. It would seem illogical, for example, to expect the ten-year-old to retire on the eve of his eleventh birthday as a fully functioning concrete thinker to awaken as a youngster capable of formal (abstract) thought. Illogical, yes; and, Piaget was, at the very least, logical. He also cautioned that some adults never reach the stage of formal operations in which they can deal with abstractions and are able to hypothesize, anticipate consequences, and perceive both the distant past and the possible future. Even those who become formal thinkers will revert to a lower cognitive level when confronted with unfamiliar material. Toepfer (1980) found that fewer than 20% of the youngsters who complete the eighth grade are capable of functioning at the level of formal operations.

So, in the middle school there are both concrete and formal thinkers. The youngsters who function at the formal operations level can plan ahead for many weeks or months. The concrete operations youngster can plan ahead for only a day or so. The student who functions at the formal operations level can follow logically from a basic premise to a conclusion; the concrete operations youngster cannot. The formal operations student is not dependent on being able to see, hear, taste, touch, or smell materials or in having immediate experiences with them in order to engage in mental manipulations; the concrete operations student is bound by direct experiences.

Many of the instructional materials available to grades six, seven, and eight are appropriate only for the formal thinker — the clear minority of the school population. Why is this true? Are those who select materials under the misconception that all eleven-year-olds are automatically at the level of abstract thinking known as formal operations? Is it possible that those who select materials have been deluded into believing that students need to "stretch to the materials" rather than having the materials fit students? What are the implications of young adolescents' mental development for exploration?

Emotional Development

Because young adolescents are neither children nor adults, their emotional behavior vacillates. They find themselves in a sort of "no-man's land." They are often told that they are too young for certain things and, in the next moment, they are ordered to act their ages — that they are too old to exhibit certain types of behavior. In truth, they are acting their age. A young adolescent's behavior may border on the ridiculous one moment and then reflect amazing insight the next.

Early adolescents have a finely-honed sense of justice from the standpoint of absolutes — things are either black or white with no shades of gray. Many middle level teachers have found (much to their horror) that a class will align with another student and against the teacher if the group perceives that the teacher has treated the student unfairly. They tend to oversimplify solutions to complex social and political problems — i.e., wars could be ended if the leaders of both sides would sit down with a snack and a soft drink and just agree to end the fighting (Thornburg, 1983).

Middle school students are very sensitive. They are quite conscious of the physical changes they are undergoing; they are anxious to be just like everyone else and to prevent anyone — even their parents — from attempting to single them out as different. They are aware that they are not as attractive as they might have been as young children, and they are not only sensitive to every real (or imagined) slight, but they may continue to be upset for some time to come. Many adults can still remember a hurting remark or action that embarrassed them and scarred them emotionally during their early adolescent years. The persons who were responsible for inflicting such emotional pain may never have been aware of the damage caused by their actions

Middle schoolers react to being hurt emotionally in a variety of ways. It is acceptable for male and female children to cry. It is usually perfectly acceptable for the female to weep as the result of physical or emotional pain. The male is sometimes expected to be stoic — to "be a man!" Or he may be told, "Don't be a sissy!" It is considered a disgrace for an adolescent male to weep in public — except in situations involving the death of a family member, an extremely close friend, or a beloved pet. This may partially explain why so many more beds in the psychiatric units of hospitals are occupied by males than by females.

Middle school students laugh a lot. They laugh when nothing is funny — at least not funny to adults. A large, noisy insect fluttering from light fixture to light fixture during a religious service can send both males and females into gales of laughter. They love jokes that may be quite obvious to adults, puns that border on the absurd, and "knock-knock" jokes that rely on far-fetched relationships. Ethnic, moron, and elephant jokes seem to make the rounds of each generation of early adolescents.

Social Development

Peers are an increasingly influential group in the lives of early adolescents. Middle schoolers will go to great lengths to be part of the group to which they aspire membership. At times their parents may not approve of the group. They may express concern — but this is done at the risk of making the group appear even more attractive to the youngster. The behavior of the peer group may even be the complete opposite of the normal behavior of the youngster. The group may occasionally border on delinquency.

Some youngsters who were enrolled in classes for the gifted during the elementary grades will go to extremes to be "just average" at the middle school level. In fact, some will deliberately seek the company and social interaction of students their parents would reject — *C* or *D* recipients — just so that they will not be singled out as "different."

Girls' groups are usually smaller in number and are much more likely to be short-lived than are boys' groups. Girls' groups usually consist of an even number of members (so that it will be possible to organize in pairs). Girls' groups may last only until new, more interesting girls move into the neighborhood, and new groups are formed. Boys' groups may last not only for the adolescent years but for the remainder of the boys' lives. Boys' groups are usually centered around the boys' mutual enjoyment of an activity, such as basketball, video games, working on motors, playing war, watching action movies, or exploring the uses of computers. The leader of the boys' group is the individual who most personifies the norm of the group, not necessarily the outstanding performer of the activity.

What about adults in the early adolescent's life? Parents are still important, and so are many other adults. These youngsters need adults who are supportive of them and who understand that they need much more freedom and greater independence than they had as children. It isn't easy to know when their youngsters require some degree of support and when they need to have freedom equal to that afforded adults. They admire adults who are fair, consistent, and willing to listen. They reject adults who are judgmental or impatient, or who want to be their "buddies."

These youngsters will go to great lengths to keep from being embarrassed in the presence of their peers. Many a teacher who has challenged a less-than-willing student has been met with brick-wall resistance. Youngsters learn early that the best defense is a good offense. They challenge teachers with one of the many means open to them — an arrogant shrug, expletives, a glare that communicates their feelings, or even physical action.

Most young adolescents undergo the many changes typical of their developmental group without a great degree of "storm and stress." Most develop into fairly well-adjusted adolescents and later, into normal, functioning adults. This has been the case in spite of the fact that educators, psychologists, and sociologists have tended to ignore this age group until the last few decades. We now know more about this age group than we have ever known and have fewer reasons not to apply this knowledge to developing school programs.

THE NATURE OF THE MIDDLE SCHOOL

Those of us who work in middle schools often hear remarks from the lay public such as "middle school? Don't you really mean `junior high'?" or "Oh, it is just another name for junior high!" The confusion is probably the fault of those of us who advocate the middle school as a viable alternative to other organizational plans that house grades six through eight. We have not been diligent enough in educating our professional colleagues or the lay public as to the differences between the junior high as it is generally operated and the middle school that is advocated.

George (1986) delineated the differences between the proposed middle school and the typical elementary and high school in Figure 1. Over the years these characteristics that make the middle school "separate and unique" have come to be accepted as the components of the middle school concept. They define the "authentic" middle school.

Figure 1

THE MIDDLE SCHOOL—
SEPARATE AND UNIQUE

	Elementary	Middle School	High School
1. Student/Teacher relationships	Parental	Advisor	Random
2. Teacher preparation	Child-oriented generalist	Flexible resource	Discipline specialist
3. Teacher organization	Self-contained	Interdisciplinary teams	Departments
4. Student grouping	Chronological	Multi-age	Subject
5. Curriculum	Skills	Exploration	Depth
6. Instruction	Teacher-directed	Balance	Student-directed
7. Building organization	Single classrooms	Team area	Department
8. Schedule	Self-contained	Block	Periods

Adapted and used with the permission of Paul S. George

Middle schools are neither senior versions of the elementary school nor junior versions of the high school — although the *nontraditional* junior high school and the middle school have many common characteristics.

How is the "authentic middle school" different from the organizational level that precedes and that which follows it?

Differences Concerning Teachers

A. Student-teacher relationships. The middle school is student-centered, and all adults in the school fulfill a counseling role. The school encourages the availability of an adult to whom each youngster can turn with problems or for advice. Teacher advisory plans provide reference groups that help early adolescents explore problems. This is different from the role of the elementary teacher who may serve "in loco parentis," in the place of the parent. This advisor role in the middle school is also different from that of the high school teacher who is a specialist in a particular content area and whose relationship with students is dependent to a great extent on the ability and interest of the student in the teacher's field of specialization.

B. Teacher preparation. Perhaps the greatest need in any middle school is to have teachers who understand the development of the students to be served and who are knowledgeable about the content that is appropriate for these youngsters. Middle school teachers must be aware of the wide range of differences in intellectual development as well as those related to the variance in physical, social, and emotional development. Until the 1970s there were only a few programs designed specifically for the preparation of middle school teachers. These pioneer programs were in operation before their state education agencies approved special certification requirements for teachers in the middle grades. The developers of these programs identified the important characteristics, knowledge, and skills needed by middle school teachers.

Middle school teachers can neither limit themselves to developing expertise in one specific content field nor to becoming generalists who "know a little bit about a lot of things." Perhaps the most appropriate description of an effective middle school teacher is as a "flexible resource" (George, 1986). It's impossible for any teacher to know all there is to know about any one content field. One can expect, however, that the teacher might be aware of a variety of informational resources. This helps the teacher to suggest many sources so that students can locate material about specific subjects. The need then is for a teacher with some depth in at least two content fields, who can recognize a connection among the various subject areas, and who is knowledgeable about sources of materials that may provide answers to problems posed in the process of instruction.

C. Teacher organization. Another distinguishing feature of the middle school relates to teacher organization. Interdisciplinary teaming involves a group of teachers (usually 3 or 4) who plan instruction for a group of students (usually 75-100). Because this group of teachers work with the same students, it is possible for them to relate and integrate content, share information about students, and to collaborate in student evaluation and in parent conferences. Early adolescents have not reached the level of intellectual development at which they are capable of identifying relationships among the various content areas when taught separately. It becomes the responsibility of the team to help students discover that knowledge is interrelated.

For years many educators believed that team teaching required working together in the same physical space. Some even went so far as to emphasize the need for large groups of students in auditorium-sized instructional settings with one teacher at a time serving as master (or lead) teacher and other instructional personnel (including certified teachers) serving as aides. The organizational strategies expressed by Trump and Baynham (1961), who advocated differentiated staffing and large blocks of instructional time were influential.

A more widely accepted approach to team organization is *interdisciplinary planning*. In this type of organization a group of teachers from various content areas are assigned the same group of students. These teachers integrate content by deliberate planning of related activities. Such an arrangement might focus on a topic such as the history of the state. The social studies teacher may take the lead, calling meetings, helping teammates plan presentations in the other content fields that can be associated with the study of the history and geography of the state. This might include the literary figures who were/are natives of the state, the nature of their work (language arts), the state's natural resources, and the impact of the states's geographic location and social conditions on the types of resources available (science), and the apportionment of political representatives in local, state, and national governmental bodies (mathematics).

The team might use grids such as those in Figures 2 and 3 (adapted from Compton, 1984) to plan the integration of content. (The information presented here is meant to be illustrative, and the reader should recognize that not *all* content fields can be included in the integration process at all times).

FIG 2: A HUMANITIES GRID FOR CURRICULUM PLANNING

Topic	Art	Language	Music	Social Studies
Who am I?				
How man has lived in groups				
How man developed governmental systems				
How man has communicated				
How man developed transportation				
How man developed industrialization				
How man developed technology				
International Relationships				

FIG 3: A TECHNOLOGY GRID FOR CURRICULUM PLANNING

Topic	Industrial Arts	Home Living	Mathematics	Science
Measurement				
Natural Resources U.S.				
Natural Resources World				
Plant Life Regional				
Plant Life U.S.				
Animal Life Regional				
Animal Life U.S.				
Ecology				
Genetics				

Differences Concerning Students

A. Student grouping. Another area of difference among elementary, middle, and senior high schools is the way students are grouped for instruction. These differences stem mainly from the fact that students at the three levels are so different. But it must be remembered that the roots of the differences in the three types of organization also lie in the history of the American educational enterprise. Traditionally and legally, young children begin formal education because of their chronological ages. Kindergarten is for five-year-olds. A child must have celebrated his/her sixth birthday before a certain calendar date in order to enter first grade. Youngsters who progress normally through the grades are seven years old in grade two; eight, in third grade; etc.

By the time students reach high school they have been through a selection process that eliminates (psychologically, if not physically) the lowest achieving students who are not expected to go to college. College-bound students are counseled into certain courses and may have the opportunity to select a class section, an instructor, or even a specific course — such as French I or advanced band.

The middle school population includes students who are not only of varying ages, but they are also at different ability levels and represent a variety of interests. During their years in the middle school students may have the final opportunity they will ever have during their school careers to learn with a group that is scheduled to meet together because the members of the group share a common interest. A group that is based on shared interest may include students from any or all of the levels in the middle school. Some schools encourage multi-age groupings.

B. Curriculum. The elementary school's major focus is the development of skills — those that seem to have always been associated with it — reading, writing, and arithmetic and some of the skills that are becoming the "new basics."

The middle school also focuses on skills. It is important that the middle school continue the development of skills introduced at the elementary level. Every student needs to develop further the various language skills as well as other communication abilities. Some authors offer lists of skills to be developed during the middle school years — reading and related study skills; speaking, questioning, and listening skills; writing skills; quantitative skills (such as computation); using major learning tools; and, problem solving and other higher intellectual processes (Alexander & George, 1981).

But the middle school curriculum includes more than the development of skills that will serve as tools for learning for the remainder of one's life. No school board and no board of trustees will tolerate the absence of language arts, mathematics, social studies, and science. These areas have been labelled "core," "academic," or as Alexander and others (1969) referred to them as the "area of organized knowledge." All too often these content areas are emphasized to the near exclusion of the others because they are the areas included on achievement tests. And few educators will advocate the elimination of these "big four." Our plea is for the selection of appropriate topics within these content areas — and for exploiting them as exploratory areas.

The major characteristic that distinguishes the middle school from the other two levels is this emphasis on exploration. Students are given the opportunity to gain new knowledge and to try out new skills and abilities in an atmosphere free of the fear of failure. Students can have some experience with new material and new content before they are required to specialize at the senior high school level. They will be much more aware of their strengths and weakness and their interests before they and their parents are required to make decisions about the direction their educational careers will take in high school and beyond. For many students exploration at the middle school level will be the only opportunity they will have to try out content and skills of their own choice.

C. Instruction. Because of the immaturity of elementary school children, *most* of the instruction is planned by teachers, although many exceptional teachers involve students in planning from the earliest years. As youngsters progress from kindergarten through fifth grade they become much more capable of involvement in determining instructional activities. They are capable of teaching themselves and in aiding in teaching their peers.

When youngsters enter the middle school they not only can share the planning of instruction with their teachers, they can select the content they want to learn, plan methods and activities to accomplish their goals, and evaluate their own progress. Middle school students of all ability levels can take some responsibility for independent study — to varying degrees and for varying periods of time.

At the high school level there are fewer reluctant learners (because many have dropped out), and many teachers take less responsibility for directing learning. If a student applies himself/herself and is able to do well on teacher-made and standardized tests, teachers and administrators are relatively satisfied. If students do not do well, it is they who are considered lazy or lacking in motivation. Often students who do poorly are channelled into technical/vocational programs in the attempt to provide them with work skills before they actually withdraw from formal education.

Differences Concerning the School Environment.

A. Building organization. The nature of the student to be served, the nature of the curriculum, and the types of instruction provided all come together to have an impact on the nature of the building organization at the three educational levels.

In the elementary school the individual classroom teacher is responsible for teaching almost all areas. It is logical then for teachers and their classes to be assigned to a specific classroom in which they remain for most of the day. Instructional materials and supplies are stored in that self-contained classroom. The teacher's last name may be displayed prominently on the classroom door. Other students at the same grade level are likely to be housed in adjacent or nearby rooms, and teachers in these classrooms will have similar facilities.

Interdisciplinary teaming at the middle school level requires a building organization quite different from that of the elementary school. Although teachers may spend most of their time in a specific classroom, students move within a group of three, four, or five classrooms known as the "team area." In schools built for the team plan open space or flexible areas may be assigned as team areas, and team names or logos may appear on classroom doors.

Departmental areas — clusters of rooms equipped for the teaching of science, for example — represent the mode in the high school. Students move from one area of the building to another regardless of their designated year of schooling. Teachers may provide instruction for sophomores, juniors, and/or seniors during the school day.

B. School schedule. All of the characteristics attributed to the elementary school, the middle school, and the high school should be used to determine the types of instruction most appropriate for each level. Schedules should reflect instruction, not vice versa. The self-contained elementary classroom calls for a schedule determined by the teacher.

In the high school teachers are assigned to teach a single content area. Because students are expected to move from one content area to another and from one classroom to another, a schedule of separate periods is needed to accommodate such a curriculum of separate subjects that are placed in departments.

The middle school typically utilizes a team approach in which students are assigned to a group of teachers who plan most of the instructional activities. Because students are assigned to teams, large blocks of time must be available to the team. The team then divides the schedule at the team's discretion.

CHAPTER TWO
Characteristics of Exploration

Consideration of the needs and interests of students when planning curricula is not a modern notion. William T. Harris called for a humanistic approach to curriculum in the late 19th century. His work was followed by that of G. Stanley Hall and John Dewey, who used the scientific approach to child and adolescent development to fashion curricula that focused on the students (Glatthorn, 1987).

Dewey's philosophy, an outgrowth of which was the progressive education movement, permeated elementary schools by the mid 1940s. Although many of the school practices that were reported as following from Dewey's philosophy may not have been in line with his child-centered approach, the adaptation of the curriculum to make it more relevant can be attributed to his work.

As the junior high school evolved it was designed to meet the needs of early adolescents — at least as educators understood those needs. Although it adopted many of the features of the senior high school, it had some characteristics that made it distinct from the high school. One experimental feature of many junior high schools was the "core" curriculum, a problem-centered block of time. This idea continues as a viable approach and is related to the integrative approach of interdisciplinary teaming. A major difference is that teaming utilizes more than one teacher whereas a single teacher was responsible for the core block.

Although there has been much dissatisfaction with the junior high school because few programs were designed to meet student needs, the exploratory program has been considered to be one of its more successful components. Many junior high school faculties found that they had to fight to preserve an exploratory program in light of the wave of curricular "reform" that followed the launching of *Sputnik*. The academic subjects were given greater emphasis and exploratory subjects came to be looked on more as frills. Many school officials supported the elimination of these non-essential subjects and a return to the "basic skills" with the notion that by eliminating these courses, time could be devoted to those content areas that would prepare future scientists and mathematicians. We needed more of such specialists who would be able to restore our country to the forefront of the space race, many said. Even today most middle schools still do not include adequate exploratory courses in the curriculum.

As Eichhorn (1980) stated, middle schools are not the result of dissatisfaction with the *concept* of the junior high school as an intermediate level of school organization as much as they are the response to the failure of junior high programs to meet the needs of its students. There are data that indicate sixth graders can benefit from a program housing seventh and eighth grades; ninth graders, on the other hand, seem to feel more at home in the senior high school (Alexander, et al., 1969).

One of the first lighthouse middle school programs was established by Eichhorn in the Upper St. Clair (Pennsylvania) public schools. The curriculum combined several content areas into instructional blocks. One of these blocks, entitled "physical-cultural curriculum" included the fine arts, physical education, practical arts, and cultural studies (understanding of the people of a region and their way of life). The exploratory program was included in this curricular component (Eichhorn, 1972).

Alexander and his co-authors (1969) advocated a middle school program based on similar components of the design used in the Upper St. Clair Schools. They supported a personal development area that included learning activities related to the individual's development, exclusive of those activities "directly aiming at his (her) development of cognitive abilities" (p. 65). This curricular area would include opportunities for counseling, development of values, health, physical development, and activities of particular interest to students. Each student would be permitted to learn about areas of interest and to decide whether or not to participate in these activities for extended periods of time.

Webster's dictionary defines "exploration" as the act of looking into closely, examining carefully, and investigating. An appropriate synonym might be "discovery." The definition of exploration used in this book is as follows: *Exploration is the conscious effort of a school to provide opportunities for students to discover, in a fairly threat-free setting, their strengths, weaknesses, likes, dislikes, and potential future curriculum choices.*

This definition calls for a program that may be quite different from that provided in the junior high. Such a program is not limited only to those areas ordinarily considered to be the fine arts, home economics, industrial arts/ technology and music.

There have been many forces at work that have made the function of exploration difficult to implement. Two major ones have been the so-called "excellence" movement and the "back-to-basics" movement, which have held that the only knowledge that should be pursued is that in the so-called "hard" subjects. Groups that advocate this approach seem to ignore that which makes one truly "human" — those content areas designed to develop the person.

The middle school is the right time for students to discover — discover themselves, their abilities, interests, and limitations; discover others and examine the values, mores, and customs of the dominant society as well as those of other societies and cultures; and, discover one's environment and our interdependence with it. Essential objectives by any measure.

Discovering Self

Exploration, according to NASSP's Council on Middle Level Education, is not unique to middle school students. All children are curious about themselves and their potential. However, during the early adolescent years, youngsters are persons "in search of personality. Their search for identity drives them to discover not only who they are, but to define who and what they want to and can become" (p. 9).

One of the most difficult tasks middle school students encounter is that which requires them to understand the persons they are becoming. They must learn to cope with changing bodies that no longer obey previous commands and are no longer well-coordinated. They experience feelings that they have never had before and yearnings that they don't know quite how to satisfy. Their energy levels may be depleted quite easily. They share the hopes and aspirations of their parents and other significant adults in their lives and yet, they yearn for independence. They are influenced by media and by their friends. They desperately search for an understanding of who they are and who they may become. They seek means of trying out new skills and new concepts without failing in the eyes of adults, or more importantly, while being observed by their peers.

Through exploration students are able to assess their strengths and weaknesses, to identify likes and dislikes and areas in which they may eventually want to develop expertise. The middle school should help these youngsters discover those skills and abilities that should be fostered and extended because of the personal satisfaction students may gain from them. By the same token, limitations may also be discovered and decisions made as to whether or not overcoming these limitations may be worth the effort required. The student who discovers the ability to master a foreign language may want to continue the development of these language skills in future years. On the other hand, the student who, on short exposure, finds no facility for a foreign language will very likely avoid further study.

No one can teach students to understand themselves. We can only make available a non-threatening environment in which they can begin to experience the changes that are taking place. There has never been an individual exactly like each of the youngsters with whom we work and live — and there never will be this same person again. Helping early adolescents to become acquainted with the persons they are now and the ones they may become in the future is a major task for the middle school.

Discovering Others

Middle schoolers also need to understand and participate in the world outside of their own families. They are interested in and concerned about their peers and the community. At this stage of development they can begin to understand and appreciate the diversity of values and feelings represented in the school population. We do a disservice to students when we limit their perceptions to only one side of an issue. While the school does not "teach" particular values it should help students to become aware of options and recognize that others hold different views. They must learn to respect the rights of others who believe differently. For many youngsters these opportunities will be the opening of vistas previously unknown and, for many, unimaginable.

For these early adolescents, who tend to see simple solutions to complex problems, to understand that others may feel very strongly about their own feelings and values and that they may be unwilling to surrender their viewpoints may be a major task. These same youngsters who feel that world leaders may be able to meet for an afternoon snack to work out the future of all people may begin to see that there is much more to compromise than meets the eye.

Discovering One's Environment

Exploration at the middle school level is also designed to help students discover the world in which they live. Part of this discovery is the interrelatedness of all knowledge. Exploratory activities should cut across artificial content boundaries and be inherent in all subjects.

The opportunities available to each of us are so vast that we would never have enough years to discover all of them. It is only as adults that we understand the plethora of options available — and we also begin to despair of the limited time available in our lifetimes to explore these options. It is important to help students to exercise wisely and without threat the options available to them. They should be free to select the "wrong" ones as well as those that are deemed suitable.

Too many adults are unaware of the beautiful and exciting world in which we live. Through a rich exploratory program middle school students may expand their understanding of their world — from local, regional, national, and international perspectives. In addition, they may begin to see that there is not only a world that can be seen easily, but there is a vast expanse beyond our planet that man is only beginning to explore. There is also a world within each of us and about us that is visible only to the most sophisticated microscope. This may indeed be the world we need to explore now.

Categories of Exploration

In an ideal middle school there would be no artificial divisions known as subjects or content areas. Capelluti and Brazee (1992) cautioned about accepting the assumption that not all curricular areas have equal importance and that the so-called "academics" are of greatest value.

An interdisciplinary approach to the curriculum has been supported by many middle school proponents from the earliest days of the middle school movement (Alexander, Williams, Compton, Hines, Prescott, and Kealy, 1969; Eichhorn, 1972). In recent years those who are concerned about an appropriate curriculum for the middle school have proposed that in order to truly meet the needs of early adolescents an interdisciplinary approach is absolutely essential (Arhar, 1992; Davies, 1992; Carnegie Council on Adolescent Development's Task Force on Education of Young Adolescents, 1989; McDonough, 1991). The educational benefits of interdisciplinary teaming have been documented by Davies (1992); Erb and Doda (1990), Vars (1987), and Lounsbury (1992).

Beane (1990) proposed a middle school curriculum organized around a progressing series of themes and issues that reflect the developmental character-istics and needs of students. He pointed out the problems one encounters in life are not neatly categorized into the realm of one or more content areas. This approach is supported by Messick and Reynolds (1992) who stated, "...Rel-evance is increased when students can, first, apply knowledge to real life situations that by nature are themselves interdisciplinary, and, second, carry out problem-solving that requires addressing content from different perspectives" (p. 164).

Utilization of the thematic approach in a ninth grade unit has been described by Carper (1991). Many hands-on experiences that lend themselves to a specific content area and require individual and group efforts are offered. An even more extensive merging of content areas and exploratory experiences is described by Springer (1992). In this program seventh graders spend their entire day and year with a two-and-a-half person team studying every aspect of the environment and utilizing field sites extensively.

Although many authors are fully in accordance with the prospect of a curriculum based on themes that are both useful and meaningful to students, they also recognize that the implementation of such a curriculum may be many years down the road. Not only must middle school educators embrace the concept, it must be understood and supported by administrators, lay groups, and school reformers. This takes time.

We are reminded of the slowness of change to interdisciplinary teaming. Eichhorn (1966) advocated this type of organization. Alexander and McEwin (1989) reported that the percentage of departmentalized programs in grade six had increased from 43% to 46% over the past twenty years. The percentage in grades seven and eight had actually dropped from 82% to 69% in grade seven and from 82% to 73% in grade eight. This is far from heartening. More than three out of five youngsters in the seventh grade and seven out of ten eighth graders are in schools that utilize a high school type of instructional organization based on the university model that dates back to medieval times. As Paul George has often said, anyone who thinks that middle school youngsters can benefit from a school organization from medieval times, just doesn't understand these youngsters. The studies of Epstein and Mac Iver (1990) support Alexander and McEwin's findings. Most middle level schools still do not use the interdisciplinary organization. Therefore, most youngsters in grades six through eight are still being subjected to the separate subjects curriculum that is reminiscent of the 1960s — or 1940s.

The authors' intention is to make this volume helpful for teachers who work in the middle schools of the 1990s. Some who will use it are parts of effective interdisciplinary teams; others are still in distinct departmental organizations. The challenge we face as authors is to provide information and activities that can be used by both groups of teachers and all those in between. It is our hope that creative teachers, regardless of the school organization in which they work, will recognize the interrelatedness of the activities suggested by the authors. For purposes of easy access, however, activities are categorized by dominant content areas. For many of the activities, categorization proved almost impossible.

The most commonly recognized category of exploration includes art, music, home living, and industrial arts/technology, computer (information) science, and possibly drama or foreign language. Because these areas have long been included in junior and senior high schools, equipment and facilities are usually available for them. It may pose a problem to convince specialists in these areas that the course content for the middle school should differ from that of the high school and should not just be watered-down high school content.

An exploratory component that is more difficult to implement is the enrichment/activities program. Mini-courses, as they are commonly called, are likely to be viewed as frills and a waste of time in an already full and busy schedule. In reality, an activities program will not only augment the academic program, it may provide for the practical application of knowledge and skills introduced but not applied in the academic program. George and Lawrence (1982) stated that there is a close positive relationship between well-designed exploratory courses and the development of skills — in other words, the greater the number of these "frills," the greater the development of skills. They emphasized as well the desirability of having each staff member participate in the exploratory program. Each leader of an activity, be this person a teacher, administrator, member of the support staff, or a volunteer from the community, should be able to identify those content areas that relate to the specific activity. For example, a leader of an activity entitled, "The American Musical Theater," should discuss the connection of Broadway musical plays to literature, drama, art, music, technology, sociology, history, economics, mathematics, and psychology. These connections might be part of the description provided for students and their parents before they indicate their choices of mini-courses.

Many authors have suggested that exploratory activities should be provided in the required content areas (Brazee, 1987; Lipsitz, 1983; Lounsbury, 1991; Merenbloom, 1988). In her study of highly successful schools for early adolescents, Lipsitz (1983) found that even in these schools the most interesting, exciting, and innovative learning experiences were provided in courses other than the academics. Many of the academic offerings were dull, non-intellectual, and dominated by activities that required students to learn by rote.

Brazee (1987) deplored the lack of exploratory activities provided through the academic areas. He stated, "If exploration is a valid concept, then we must be concerned that ALL aspects of the middle level are exploratory. Given the state of curriculum planning in middle level schools, it is obvious that this expanded vision of what exploration *can* be does not yet exist" (p. 33).

In Chapter Three ways in which teachers of language, social studies, mathematics, and science might include exploratory activities within those required content areas are discussed. It will be apparent that it is difficult to categorize some of these activities under a single content area. One of the activities suggested, for example, is "electronic language." It was placed in a section related to language, but it could as easily have been discussed under the general headings of *mathematics, science,* and *social studies*.

Readers are urged to examine all sections not just those related to a specific teaching area. Most of the topics could be included in more than one of the subject areas. The identification of these activities is intended to be suggestive. Creative teachers will go well beyond those included to many more, some of which can be shared with team members.

Chapter Four is a discussion of exploratory activities that can be provided through "special" content areas — art, music, home living, technology, health, etc. Again it was difficult to assign some of these activities to a specific area. Many cut across the artificial barriers that define these areas. Most of the suggested topics will also be applicable to academic courses as well.

In Chapter Five activities and mini-courses are discussed in some detail. Again, these are not meant to be exhaustive. Teachers will want to add to the list.

CHAPTER THREE

Exploration Through Required Content Courses

Although content in academic courses is often prescribed by state and local policy or standardized tests, there are many routes to the mastery of this content — and exploration can be addressed through some of those routes. Many examples are offered in this chapter, but this collection of questions and suggested activities is not meant to be exhaustive. We hope readers will draw on their own backgrounds and experiences to identify additional activities suitable to their school situations. These suggestions are not intended to take the place of content in required areas only to enhance or supplement it.

LANGUAGE ARTS

Perhaps the most basic content area is language arts. There are so very many activities that lend themselves to the study of language. The questions and activities below are all exploratory in nature and will encourage critical thinking.

Origins of the Language

When confronted with the question, "Why and when did human beings first feel the need to have spoken or written language?" Middle schoolers may find their curiosities peaked. There is, of course, no precise answer. It might be fun to speculate on ways people communicated before language was developed. What is a language? How many languages are there? (At last count there were nearly 3,000 separate languages, and this doesn't include those dedicated to computers.) Youngsters may attempt to communicate with one another by any means possible without using written or spoken language. Why did it become necessary to go beyond gestures to depend on written or spoken language? Because middle grade youngsters are creative and have keen senses of humor, they may delight in developing a folk tale (a lá Aesop's fables) to explain how language began.

In addition to the 3,000 known languages there are many dialects. What is the difference between a language and a dialect? What are some examples of dialects?

Why is there no common language that is used throughout the world? Is there a single language that is coming into international use? What or who determines which language that would be? Has there ever been an attempt to develop a new language that would be used by all countries? What was it and what happened to it? Is there a need to develop such a language? What signs and symbols have come into international use that can be interpreted by people throughout the world?

The language that is used by a majority of the American people is a version of English that has evolved over the years. How is it different from that spoken and written by the people who live in Great Britain? Australia? All languages change — for better or for worse. Words come into common usage that may not have been used by previous generations — or that may have earlier been considered to be misuses of other words. How have some of the common expressions such as "raining cats and dogs" come into usage? The meanings of some words change over time. Early adolescents can probably give many examples.

What elements (such as nouns and verbs) are common to all languages? Which elements are common to only a certain group of them? What languages are used by subgroups within the broader culture?

The Science of Speaking

The human body includes those organs necessary for speech — the larynx, the vocal chords, the lungs, the tongue, the hard and soft palates, and the lips. The process of forming sound and enunciating syllables is a conscious act and follows a required sequence. The process does not vary regardless of whether the speaker is British, Russian, Korean, or some other nationality. Young adolescents could well explore many questions relating to speaking such as the following.

— What causes speech impediments?
— How do these impediments affect speech?
— Can they be overcome?
— Can speech occur if any of these organs are damaged?
— How is artificial speech accomplished?
— Why does one's voice sound different when heard on a recording than from the standpoint of the person speaking?
— Why are some voices more distinguishable than others?
— Why do the "voices" of robots sound different from those of people?

Language as Cultural Identity

Are Germans arrogant? Are Italians highly excitable? Are the French great lovers? Or is it the sound of their languages that make them appear that way? Why does Castilian Spanish sound different from the recordings used for the teaching of Spanish? Students may begin their study of this topic by exploring the accents of New Englanders as compared with those of people from the deep South in our own country. Do people who live in Alabama sound different from those who live in Virginia even though both are southern states.

Do Americans and the British speak the same language? What did Prime Minister Winston Churchill mean when he said that the greatest barrier between the two nations was their language? Why do people — especially older immigrants — tend to continue to use their native languages even after they settle in a new country? Sometimes people who come from other countries settle in areas of cities inhabited by other immigrants from the same country. How would one feel if one moved to a country in which everyone else spoke Russian? Why does the average American resist learning a foreign language? How do you feel when you are around people who speak a common foreign language that you do not understand? Do you feel that it is a deliberate attempt to exclude you from the conversation? Students may explore these and other questions in order to gain some understanding of the importance of language.

The Language of Music

Many people consider music to be an international language. The presence of a distinct martial beat arouses people to march and follow a parade. Slow, deliberate music played in a minor key causes people to feel sad because this type of music is often played at funerals. Is this true regardless of the nationality of the audience? Italian (from Latin) is the language used to give directions in music. Why is that language used? What do the terms mean? If you make an audio recording of a television program, can you listen to it and determine the type of action that is occurring without seeing it? How does music set the mood? How is background music used in propaganda films? Students might write a story or use an existing one and select background music to accompany it.

Electronic Language

The invention of the computer has made possible many types of electronic language. Computer-generated language has become a part of our everyday lives. Transportation systems such as rapid transit networks use electronic language to provide announcements to passengers. Electronic language in automobiles remind motorists to fasten seat belts, to close doors, and to turn headlights on or off. Even soft drink machines have been programmed to communicate with prospective buyers. Electronic language may be oral or written. Many years ago at Yale University the "talking typewriter" was used as an instructional device for elementary students. At the time it was considered the harbinger of the teaching machine, which was prophesied as the ultimate replacement for the classroom teacher.

Middle school students might attempt to find answers to questions such as the following:

— How is electronic language produced? Why do some responses sound like machines while others sound like human voices?
— Why are male voices more often chosen for recordings?
— Can machines be programmed to "think" and respond accordingly?
— What practical uses for electronic language do you foresee for your home? At your future workplace? In the entertainment industry? In the public safety arena? As a means of gathering information?

English as an Evolving Language

Specialists in the development of language tell us that English as we know it comes from many other languages — not a mixture as much as a combination of words and phrases from other language systems. Some of these are borrowed from the Germanic category; some from the Romance languages; some from Slavic; and some from Asian systems.

English today is unlike *Olde English,* and it is quite different from the language of colonial America. Youngsters might examine *Beowulf* in an attempt to understand the story. Shakespeare's works present a different challenge for middle school students as do the works of Thomas Paine and Benjamin Franklin. Students may be interested in the works of E.E. Cummings and Ogden Nash and the unique writing styles of these authors. Students may be intrigued with the variations in spelling used by Thomas Jefferson — and from that exposure become more aware of the necessity for spelling and grammar rules.

Most middle school students enjoy *Archy and Mehitabel* by Don Marquis. They are amused by the notion that Archy, a cockroach, uses a typewriter to produce the manuscript by jumping from key to key. All letters are lower case because a cockroach cannot hold down the "shift" key and press another key simultaneously. They might want to try keying a story on the computer using only one finger.

Many words are added to our language each year as the result of technology, scientific breakthroughs, and sociological change. Students may want to develop a list of words used in their everyday lives or selected from the local newspaper. Were these words in use (as reflected in the dictionary) ten years ago? Was the word used with a different meaning then? What about *stoned, crack, mainline, gay, input, cool, bad,* or *AIDS*? How do new words get added to our dictionary? How is the preferred meaning determined? How does one know which one is the preferred meaning? How is the language of origin of a word indicated in the dictionary? What do you think English will be like fifty years from now? Will we still need to know how to write and how to spell?

Argot — Designing Your Own Language

Each generation of middle level students seems to rediscover various forms of argot. These are languages students develop, adapt, and/or adopt in order to communicate with one another with a reasonable assurance that adults will not understand what they are saying. What adult today was not fluent at one time in "igpay atinlay" (pig Latin)? Many other types of argot have been used through the years. Some youngsters have learned to use sign language for the same reasons. Students may try to develop their own private languages. (This is a particularly good exploratory activity for boys because boys usually have greater interest and skill in this area than do girls.) It may prove to be a way "to snatch" the interest of boys during a period of their educational careers in which they may be turned off by English (grammar).

Secret Codes

Many middle-aged adults can recall with nostalgia the codes used by such radio and television heroes as Captain Marvel, Roy Rogers, and others. The announcer on these programs would encourage the purchase of "decoder rings" or the "hero's" code book. At times "secret messages" were presented over the air, and only those faithful fans who had purchased the decoding devices (usually through submitting the required number of cereal box tops and a small amount of cash) were able to receive the messages. Many of these so-called messages read as if they had been extracted from "fortune cookies," but the recipients of the coded materials were excited to receive them and kept their contents secret.

Codes may be written or they may be transmitted by sound. Ancient tribes used drums to communicate messages. Later, with the invention of the Morse code, a more sophisticated "sound message" system came into being. The principle, however, was the same. Frequencies of sound relayed the message. Some students may wish to learn the Morse code and practice it with classmates and/or friends.

They may want to explore codes more thoroughly. How have codes been used through the history of man? Who were the first military groups to use codes? What is meant by SOS when it is broadcast from a ship? What does "mayday" mean when used by the pilot of a plane? What was the first ship to use the emergency signal in Morse code? What kinds of codes were used by American Indians? By African tribes?

Some youngsters may try to develop a system of communication that utilizes pictures or symbols. Certain words and ideas will be essential. Some means must be developed for encoding and decoding. Once the code has been determined, students can practice it by writing letters or stories. A wise middle school teacher will encourage rather than restrict such activities — even if the code is put to questionable uses.

Story Telling

The earliest means of relating history was probably by an adult family member telling anecdotes to a child from the same family. Sometimes the facts were changed slightly to make the story more interesting. Storytellers were very special members of tribes — often revered by all members. Parents, grandparents, and other adults have, for centuries, held youngsters spellbound with their stories of heroism and daring.

There is an art to story telling — an art that can be developed and nurtured in students. This skill may help all students at all ability levels to work with peers as well as with younger students. Students who have had little success with other types of language experiences may excel here.

Middle level students may wish to become acquainted with skilled story tellers in the community. When they have the basic skill, they may want to practice using fellow students as audiences. They may even decide to form a club for story tellers and volunteer to tell stories in nursery schools, hospital pediatric wards, and/or in homes for the elderly. Story telling as a career or avocation may also be a topic of exploration.

American Legends

There are legends in all cultures. The Greeks and Romans attributed great feats of power and heroism to gods and goddesses. The Norsemen told of the feats of Odin and Thor. The English repeat the legend of King Arthur, the knights of his round table, and of his wondrous sword, Excaliber. Robin Hood and his merry men of Sherwood Forest have been the theme of song, movie, and television series in Great Britain and in our country. Paul Bunyan, Pecos Bill, Davy Crockett, Daniel Boone, and Annie Oakley have captured the imaginations of American youngsters throughout much of our comparatively brief history. Modern legends include Bigfoot and the Abominable Snowman.

What makes a legend? What elements must be exaggerated? How superhuman must the deeds be? One might identify an incident from the local or national news and use it to develop a legend. Are women ever legendary characters? Why do some people believe that all legends are really true? Why do legends survive from one generation to another? Do people of various countries borrow legends from another country? Are legendary deeds ever attributed to real people such as George Washington, Abraham Lincoln, or Jim Bowie?

Poetry

Some people believe that poetry is written by serious old men who struggle to make iambic pentameter rhyme. The early minstrels of medieval times sang rhyming poetry to communicate the news of the day. The *Sonnets to the Portuguese,* which express the great love of Elizabeth Barrett and Robert Browning, are romantic enough to thrill even the least impressionable early adolescent. Epic poems provide enough danger and adventure for the imagination of any middle level student. Boys love *Casey at the Bat.* Because boys are more likely to enjoy humor than are girls, they are more likely to enjoy the poetry of Ogden Nash. Limericks are humorous poems that can be used to help youngsters write their own poetry. The teacher must be cautious to avoid their exposure to the more bawdy ones that are available in many books of limericks.

Youngsters may select a news or sports story and rewrite it in a poetic format. Once youngsters experience the fun of poetry they may be more open about expressing their own experiences, thoughts, and feelings through poetry.

Early adolescents should be helped to understand that not all poetry must rhyme. Special attention should be given to blank or free verse.

Who-Dunnits

A popular radio program that later inspired a short-lived television series was entitled, *I Love a Mystery.* This could well be the motto of middle school students. Many of them are introduced to writers of the stature of Nathaniel Hawthorne and Edgar Allen Poe during their early adolescent years. Some develop a love of mysteries that follows them the rest of their lives. The genre of the who-dunnit offers some of the same satisfaction as does the solving of a puzzle or the unraveling of a riddle — activities that interest the middle school student.

Real life mysteries are popular in the media. There are mysteries that involve crimes as well as those that are related to strange, unexplained events. Are there really such things as flying saucers? Does extra-sensory perception (ESP) really work? Are there people who can predict the future to a relatively accurate degree by looking at one's palm or by reading tea leaves left in a cup?

Youngsters enjoy being involved with mysteries. They may enjoy having the teacher read part of a mystery to them each day. They can write their own mysteries using real events reported in news magazines and local newspapers. Because of their sense of the dramatic, they may want to role-play the incident.

Perhaps the drama might be recorded on video or audio tape and shared with others. The drama might also be recorded as a radio play, complete with appropriate sound effects.

Detective stories present a form of mystery story that may be linked to a crime. Students should be encouraged to determine the sort of behavior that constitutes the commission of a crime. What motivates some people to commit crimes? What is a clue? What is the difference between a detective story and a horror story? Who are some of the world's best-known mystery writers? They may want to read *The Gold Bug* and *The Telltale Heart* to determine the elements of a mystery story and to distinguish the characteristics of a horror story.

They may enjoy developing a mystery story that uses the school as a setting. One middle school class wrote a story about the theft of a Thanksgiving turkey from the school cafeteria. They included possible suspects and the clues that might have been found.

Fun with Language

One of the interesting things about language is its potential for manipulating it for fun. This is especially true with a language such as English and its synonyms, antonyms, and homonyms. Two or more homonyms in a single sentence may be found in even the most serious works.

Introduction of the term *onomatopoeia* through a work such as Poe's poem, *The Bells,* may send youngsters in search for other examples of words that suggest their meanings. They may enjoy posting a list of examples.

Another fun exploratory activity involves tracing the origin of such expressions as "flip your wig," "sour grapes," and others. What type of significance may these expressions have had in earlier times that are quite different today. "Eating spinach will put hair on your chest" is one example that comes to mind. When one of the authors, in discussing nourishing foods with a young friend used that expression, the youngster (age 12 and female) replied, "Why on earth would I ever want to do that?"

How soon we age!

Some young adolescents enjoy drawing cartoons to illustrate metaphors. One can easily visualize a picture to demonstrate "raining cats and dogs," "working up a storm," or "busy as a bee." Even youngsters who have difficulty with most traditional language instruction will find this to be fun.

English idioms provide another enjoyable activity that could involve pictorial illustration. These might include: *I was so scared that my heart was in my throat; Tim was in the doghouse for breaking the window;* and, *Jimmy didn't perform because he got cold feet.*

Droodles show words that appear to be what they say.

BIG,

small,

W   I   D   E

are examples. Students can make their own lists $F=A=S=T=$

Careers in Language

Early adolescents are often quick to ask the question "What good will this do me when I grow up?" We respond to such query with confidence. They all use language every day and need an edge to convince their parents, sway their peers, and surprise their teachers. Some will eventually pursue careers that will depend on a knowledge of language. They may explore the requirements of such jobs as newspaper reporter, television writer, translator, textbook or novel writer, editor, environmental scanner, scientific writer, postal worker, librarian, computer programmer, lyricist, actor, cartoonist, playwright, and some occupations that may not even be dreamed of in the decade prior to the twenty-first century. It is not possible to live and work in this world without using language.

MATHEMATICS

Throughout their elementary school years, children have been developing their computational skills using the four fundamental processes with widely varying degrees of success. Teachers feel they should come to middle school ready to apply these skills to higher levels of mathematical thought. Some students would be interested in abstract concepts in geometry, algebra, measurement, and number systems. Others would be interested in applying these skills to more practical problems of banking, investing, business, taxation, and other utilitarian uses of arithmetic. However, students often show up with little interest in anything related to numbers. The National Assessment of Educational Progress has shown that 13-year-old students are inadequate in their ability to solve mathematical problems. Students in the United States ranked lowest among students their own age from five countries and four Canadian Provinces (Lapointe, Mead, & Phillips, 1989). Many middle school students lack interest in mathematics.

Drill and practice in computational skills are not exciting activities for scores of students. Too often it seems that imagination among boys and girls is laid waste in the midst of all the algorithms that are memorized to give direction in mathematics. But an exploratory approach to mathematics can bring joy to students who never expected to enjoy anything having to do with numbers. Teachers can encourage young people to explore far beyond the ideas and concepts that are traditionally presented. In this section some exciting ways students can explore with numbers, discover new relationships, and recognize new patterns are presented.

Fibonacci Numbers

Leonardo Fibonacci lived in Italy during the thirteenth century. He created a number system which has a strange relationship to the world around us. The system is easy to develop. The first two terms of the system are 0 and 1. Each succeeding term is the sum of the two terms immediately preceding it. Thus, the infinite set proceeds 0, 1, 1, 2, 3, 5, 8, 13, 21, 34. . . .

The interesting thing about this system is that many phenomena in nature are grouped into Fibonacci numbers. Leaves on trees, plants, shrubs, and vines are arranged more often in groups of 3, 5, or 8 than in other numbers. A four-leaf clover is sought as a symbol of good luck because it is rarely found. Students who build their own series of Fibonacci numbers can look around them to find how often these numbers are found. Perhaps there are other arrangements of numbers, but Fibonacci can start them exploring.

Commutative Property in Addition and Multiplication

The commutative property in mathematics simply states that in addition and multiplication it makes no difference how numbers are arranged. The sum and the product will remain the same in any case. This property is often presented just as a property of mathematics to be memorized. It can also serve to make addition and mathematics more exciting. For example, 23 + 19 + 27 can also be read as (23 + 27) + 19. The sum of 69 is much easier to read with the second arrangement of numbers than the first. Similarly, 36 + 17 + 54 + 23 can be arranged as (36 + 54) + (17 + 23). Again, the rearranged numbers show the sum to be 130 much more readily than the other ways the numbers could be ordered. In addition problems 7's and 3's, 6's and 4's, 8's and 2's, and 9's and 1's in the one's place can make addition more interesting and more fun.

In multiplication, this same property can make arriving at the product much easier and much more interesting. For example, 4 x 23 x 25 can be arranged as (4 x 25) x 23. The product of 2300 becomes readily apparent. A problem such as 4 x 6 x 25 x 3 can be changed to (4 x 25) x (6 x 3) to make the product, 1800, relatively easy to visualize. A problem, 2 x 8 x 5, can be seen as (2 x 5) x 8 to reveal 80 as the product.

Thus led in addition and multiplication, students soon find themselves manipulating numbers mentally. They become better problem solvers simply by clarifying the problem. And what is even more important, mathematics has become exciting.

Number Patterns

Students resign themselves to the fact that multiplication tables are a necessary tool. However, they typically are quite limited in scope. Patterns in numbers reach nearly infinite proportions. Two unequal factors in multiplication equally removed from a decade factor form an interesting pattern that students often find more exciting than memorizing multiplication tables.

For example: $11 \times 9 = 10^2 - 1^2 = 100 - 1 = 99$

$12 \times 8 = 10^2 - 2^2 = 100 - 4 = 96$

$13 \times 7 = 10^2 - 3^2 = 100 - 9 = 91$

$14 \times 6 = 10^2 - 4^2 = 100 - 16 = 84$

$15 \times 5 = 10^2 - 5^2 = 100 - 25 = 75$

and:

$21 \times 19 = 20^2 - 1^2 = 400 - 1 = 399$

$22 \times 18 = 20^2 - 2^2 = 400 - 4 = 396$

$23 \times 17 = 20^2 - 3^2 = 400 - 9 = 391$

$24 \times 16 = 20^2 - 4^2 = 400 - 16 = 384$

$25 \times 15 = 20^2 - 5^2 = 400 - 25 = 375$

Number patterns also appear in squaring of any number ending in five (5). The digit(s) appearing to the left of the five (5) when multiplied by the next digit(s) in sequence and then by 100 may be added to 52 or 25 to determine the square of the number.

For example: $15^2 = 1 \times 2 \times 100 + 5^2 = 200 + 25 = 225$;

or

$35^2 = 3$ x 4 x $100 + 5^2 = 1200 + 25 = 1225$

and

$115^2 = 11$ x 12 x $100 + 5^2 = 13200 + 25 = 13225$

Related to this is another pattern found in seeking the product of two two-place factors in the same decade when the sum of the digits in the one's place is ten (10). This short cut is similar to finding the square of a number ending in five (5).

For example: 23 x $27 = 20$ x $30 + (3$ x $7) = 600 + 21 = 621$

52 x $58 = 50$ x $60 + (2$ x $8) = 3000 + 16 = 3016$

and 14 x $16 = 10$ x $20 + (6$ x $4) = 200 + 24 + 224$

Another interesting number pattern emerges in squaring numbers, any numbers. If you know the square of a number, the square of the next number in sequence is the sum of the known square plus twice the square root of the previous number plus one.

For example: $13^2 = 144 + (12$ x $2) + 1 = 169$

$16^2 = 225 + (15$ x $2) + 1 = 256$

$17^2 = 256 + (16$ x $2) + 1 = 289$

$18^2 = 289 + (17$ x $2) + 1 = 324$

If you know that $40^2 = 1600$, then you know that $41^2 = 1681$ and $39^2 = 1521$.

Finally, students may notice a peculiar pattern when they examine a table of squares. The differences between successive squares seem to equal the sums of the numbers of which they are the squares and are odd numbers progressing successively by two:

Number:	1	2	3	4	5	6	7
Square:	1	4	9	16	25	36	49
Differences and sums:		3	5	7	9	11	13

and

25	26	27	28	29	30
625	676	729	784	841	900
	51	53	55	57	59

Students will perhaps find mathematics interesting and intriguing when they begin discovering the interesting patterns that are discovered as they continue to explore these fascinating relationships. School mathematics too often plays down imagination and intuition on the part of the learner. Patterns among numbers can open up mathematics to creative thought.

Some Puzzlers for Thinkers

Some students become interested in mathematics when they discover the excitement of solving problems. Listed below are a few problems that are appropriate for middle level students. These problems could be given on a weekly basis with no requirement that they be completed. Solving a puzzle without concern for a grade helps students to enjoy the powerful pieces of "equipment" their minds are.

1. If you were offered a job with a beginning salary of one penny a day that would double each day for a month, would you accept the job?

2. There could be other ways than a system of numbers to communicate numbers. Can you translate the following problem into our number system?

$ SE.ND
MO.RE
MON.EY

3. How can a 175 pound farmer take a fox, a goose, and a 25 pound sack of corn across a bridge that will hold only 200 pounds? He can take only one object across at a time and must not allow the fox to eat the goose nor the goose to eat the corn.

4. There are three jealous men and their wives who must cross a river in a two-man boat. Plan the crossing in such a way that no man has any worry about his wife.

5. There were 10 handshakers at a party. Everyone shook everyone else's hand one time. How many people were at the party?

6. Show how many different ways that 15 pennies can be put in 4 piles so that each pile has a different number of pennies.

7. Jessie was collecting $1.90 from her paper route. Mr. Hendron paid her in nickels, dimes, and quarters. How many of each coin did he give her?

8. Assume that a person can carry four days supply of food for a trip across the desert that takes six days to cross. How many persons would have to start out in order for one person to get across and for the others to get back?

9. A person went into a store and told the owner, "Give me as much money as I have and I'll spend $10 with you." He repeated this in a 2nd and 3rd store after which he had no money left. How much money did he have when he started?

10. Huntsmen always lie and noblemen always tell the truth. A stranger met three natives in a town. The first man said something the stranger didn't hear. The second man said, "He said he was a nobleman." The third man said, "The first man is a liar because he is a huntsman." How many noblemen and how many huntsmen are there?

These problems are just a few of the hundreds of problems appropriate for middle level students. It is suggested that the solutions of the problems should never be given to the students. Rather, leave the problem with them and ask questions that might keep them interested. It is the process of solving problems not the solution that motivates people to want to solve problems.

Divisibility Rules

Students spend so much time learning algorithms for division they miss the joy of mathematics. Tinnapel (1963) describes a way to determine rather quickly whether a number is divisible by 2, 3, 4, 5, 6, 8, 9, or 11. It is very easy to tell whether a number is divisible by 2. If the final digit is an even number it may be divided by 2 without a remainder.

To determine that a number is divisible by 3, total the digits and divide by 3. For example, the digits in 726 total 15 which is divisible by 3. It takes less time to total the digits in 726 than to divide 726 by 3. Middle level learners become excited to find out this information. They discover also that 267, 276, 672, and 762 are also divisible by 3 as they continue applying this divisibility rule.

In finding out that a number is divisible by 4, the learner needs to look only at the last 2 digits. If they are divisible by 4, the whole number is also. The student probably will also be able to answer why this is true. In any case this information will bring a new way to look at division.

Most students will know that a number is divisible by 5 if the final digit is either 0 or 5. They have used this information in counting money. They also have counted by 5's since the first time they played "Hide and Seek."

A number is divisible by 6 if the total of all the digits is divisible by 3 and the number is an even number. As an example, the digits 2068464 total 30 and is divisible by 3 and the entire number is divisible by 6. It is also interesting to discover that all arrangements of this number are also divisible by 6.

If the final 3 digits of any number are divisible by 8, the entire number is divisible by 8. For example, the final 3 digits of 455152 are divisible by 8. The quotient of this problem is 19. The quotient of the entire number is 56894. The middle school learner will enjoy discovering that any set of digits preceding these three digits will create a number that is still divisible by 8.

To discover whether a number is divisible by 9 is similar to the method used to find out whether a number is divisible by 3. If the sum of the digits in a number is divisible by 9 the whole number is divisible by 9. For example, the digits in 51291 total 18 which is divisible by 9. The number is also divisible by 9.

Finally, to determine whether a number is divisible by 11 is more complicated but just enough more complicated to motivate middle level learners to find out for themselves. From the sum of the odd-ordered digits subtract the sum of the even-numbered digits. If the result is either 0 or divisible by 11, the entire number is divisible by 11. For example, in the number 162679 the odd-ordered digits are 1, 2, and 7 which total 10. The even-numbered digits are 6, 6, and 9 which total 21. Subtracting 21 from 10 is -11 which is divisible by 11.

Probability and Statistics

Probability and statistics are two of the most useful applications of mathematics in daily life. They help us understand the world around us by organizing information in new ways. Traditionally these topics have not had a large part in the middle level curriculum, yet they have high interest with learners.

In one game developed by Bright and Wheeler (1981) two players use 2 red chips and 1 blue chip which are marked with an A side and a B side. The two players decide who will be Player 1 and who will be Player 2. All 3 chips are flipped at the same time. Player 2 scores one point if both red chips show A or the blue chip shows A or if both the red and blue chips show A. Otherwise Player 1 scores a point. The players play 16 rounds in a game. After three games they answer the question whether each player has an equal chance to win the game.

Interesting experiments relating to probability can be performed using dice. First, using one die, roll it 25 times and record each roll. Which number turned up most often? Were the other numbers close? Is there a pattern that has emerged? Roll the die 25 more times and record each roll. Compare these results with the first series of rolls. Are the results different? What do you think would happen after several more rolls? Follow this activity by rolling two dice. Record the results of 36 rolls on a list of all the different totals that can turn up if you roll two dice together. How do these results compare with those you obtained with one die? Roll two dice 36 more times and record the results. How do these results compare with the previous series of rolls? Middle level learners could find it exciting to develop a probability table indicating the theoretical probability of rolling every number 2-12 using two dice.

The role of probability in statistics is to provide a basis for making decisions. It is a concept that can be discovered as students explore various forms of data that surround them every day. They can discover the differences among mean, median, and mode. What are the uses of the mean, the median, or the mode in their own lives? It seems particularly meaningful for middle level students to discover their own uniqueness as they work with the concept of probability. It is entirely probable that middle grade students are normal. What is normal? Students could collect physical data from a random sample of their classmates. As they analyzed these data they would be amazed at the variability. In addition, they might come to appreciate how they fit into this wide pattern of normalcy.

Number Systems

We are so accustomed to a decimal system that many of us have a hard time believing there is any other way to count. We have counted by our fingers since we first started using numbers, and history indicates that people in Egypt and Mesopotamia had symbols for 10 earlier than 3000 BC.

However, there are ancient tribes in Australia, Africa, and South America that count by pairs in which the system is "one, two, two and one, two and two, two and two and one, two and two and two," etc. There are a few tribes which use a base three, base four, base five, and even a base six system of counting. Middle level learners might become intrigued with numbers as they explore with different bases. What are the advantages or disadvantages of different bases?

Tradition still holds us to different number systems. There is strong evidence of a duodinary system in much of what we do today. We use 12 inches in a foot to measure distance. In time we use 12 months in a year and twice 12 hours in a day. In marketing we still measure quantities in dozens and in gross measures. In England there are 12 pence in a shilling. In literature writers borrow from a base 20 to speak of a score as did Abraham Lincoln in the *Gettysburg Address.*

Going against tradition in the United States is difficult — evidence the attempts to convert to the metric system. This system of weights and measures is built on the decimal system with grams for weight, meters for distance, and liters for volume. Most names in the metric system are built by adding prefixes to these three terms. These measures are in many ways simpler than inches, pounds, and pints but, with the exception of a few beverages, tradition has kept us from changing to a metric system. Middle school learners can explore with the metric system and, at the same time, understand a lot about the behavior of people.

Finally, with the advent of rapid computers, the binary system of numbers has taken on great practical importance. Their basic operation is electrical current pulse, on or off. The numbers in the binary system are 1 and 0. The electrical pulse translates readily to these two symbols. It is interesting that this number system used by only a few ancient tribes in the world today is essential to the working of the computer which is in the midst of revolutionizing our society. What a point to ponder in exploration!

Careers in Mathematics

There is virtually no area of human existence that is not touched by mathematics in some form. Starting in the home, there is a budget to be determined. The homemaker must plan meals. There are decisions to be made about buying a new car or fixing the old one, about this summer's vacation, and putting a new roof on the house. Through it all there must be thought about eventual retirement. These decisions all involve mathematics.

Of course, there are engineers who must have an excellent background in mathematics, and architects, doctors, dentists, scientists, astronomers, pilots, economists, and industrialists must have a thorough understanding of the type of mathematics that begins in middle grades.

Many blue collar workers have to understand mathematics to do their jobs. Garage mechanics must be able to read through manuals of many makes of cars and understand different tolerances and operating levels that are described. Carpenters must be able to translate the numbers presented in blueprints before they can build a house. Plumbers and electricians must understand different codes presented from one locality to another. Truck drivers and cab drivers must be able to determine loads, distances, and hours on the road. Throughout the whole world of business there are millions of clerks, service repair people, and middle managers who each business day depend on mathematics to make themselves successful. The use of exploratory type activities will go a long way toward developing interest in mathematics, interest that will yield results in achievement.

SCIENCE

Young adolescents are concerned about the physical changes they are undergoing. This interest provides many "teachable moments" for those responsible for instruction in science. It also provides an opportunity for integrating the content of several subject areas. Topics of special interest in the sciences that are exploratory in nature are discussed in this section.

Who Am I?

Young adolescents are egocentric. They are most interested in themselves and the characteristics that make them unique. Exploratory activities might begin with questions such as: What are my vital statistics — height, weight, age? Color of hair, eyes? How do I compare with my brothers? sisters? parent(s)? What is a Christian name? Do people who are not Christians have Christian names? What is a surname? What is the origin of my surname? Does my Christian name have some meaning? Are there famous people with the same surname? The same Christian name? What famous person(s) was(were) born on the same day and the same month as I was? Who else in my school has the same birthday as mine? How am I a different person now than I was two years ago? Six years ago? Ten years ago?

Youngsters at this stage of development may also be receptive to topics that deal directly with human anatomy and physiology. For example: What are calories? How many calories does an active youngster of my height need every day? What foods provide lots of calories but very little nutrition? What types of nutrients would one find in the typical hamburger? French fries? What makes some people fat?

The function of various parts of the body may prove interesting if not overdone and not presented in a highly technical way. What does skin do? How do bones work? Why do we need muscles? Are there different types of muscles? What kinds of foods help build muscles? Bones? Why are steroids dangerous? How do you know what is in the food you buy at the grocery store? What do you need to know in order to interpret food labels?

The concept of a "biological clock" is an interesting one for students. Many organisms are active during daylight hours: robins, squirrels, bees, and some people. Others prefer nighttime hours: bats, owls, mice, and some people. Biologists refer to the way the human body controls the timing of daily activity cycles as its "biological clock." Youngsters may wish to explore their own biological clocks. At what time of day do they enjoy being most active? When do they prefer to rest? They may determine their body temperatures and pulse rates every two hours in an attempt to determine these cycles. The phenomena known as "jet lag" is brought about by a disturbance in the biological clock.

Middle school students might investigate this problem, interview someone who has experienced jet lag, and write the story for a school newspaper or television broadcast.

Race as a Factor

What does "race" mean? What are the physical components that determine the racial identity of an individual? How many racial groups are there? Can an individual represent more than one racial group? What is the largest racial group in your school? Your community? Your state? Design a chart comparing characteristics of racial groups. These are activities that can be used in middle schools to teach a variety of concepts — not the least of which is that we are all different because we come from a variety of backgrounds as well as from many different racial or ethnic groups — yet we are all very much alike.

The Role of Genetics

Part of the process of understanding oneself and one's background is gaining some knowledge of what causes a person to develop into what one is. Most of the world's population has brown eyes. There are, however, people with blue, green, gray, or hazel eyes. Youngsters may identify the determinants of eye color. What determines hair color? hair texture? degree of curliness? sex of a baby? What are genes? What is the difference between a dominant gene and a recessive gene? Why do some families have blue-eyed, blond-haired children as well as children with brown hair and brown eyes? What causes twins? Must identical twins be of the same sex? What's the difference between identical twins and fraternal twins? Are triplets determined in the same way that twins are? What about quadruplets and quintuplets? Are there certain physical defects that are more likely to be found among twins than in single children? Students might interview twins to determine what types of special relationships they may have with one another. They may also read about the Dionne or Fischer quintuplets to learn about the kinds of problems they experienced. What are Siamese twins? Why are they called that? What are the physical causes of "circus freaks" such as the bearded lady, the dog-faced boy, or the giant?

What is meant by "gestation period?" How long is the gestation period for humans? For rabbits? cats? elephants? dogs? cows? Is the gestation period likely to be longer or shorter for single children as compared to that of twins? Why? Students might interview the mother of twins in order to determine the gestation period. They may also find out about the problems of bearing twins and rearing them.

Certain physical characteristics are passed from one generation to another in a family. These traits include length of eyelashes, dimples, freckles, fixed and unfixed earlobes — to name a few. Students might find someone in their classes who has one or more of these characteristics. If there are two or more siblings in the family, how many share the particular physical characteristic?

Another trait that is shared in every family is blood type. Among humans there are four major blood types — O, AB, A and B. Youngsters may do a little detective work. They can find out their own blood types. What blood types are represented within their families? If one were to marry a person with a blood type different from theirs and there were four children born to the couple, what would the blood types of their children probably be?

Middle schoolers may wish to determine traits they share with their parents, siblings, and/or grandparents. What traits can be traced back several generations in the family?

People and the Environment

Without the intrusion of people the environment would probably be fairly safe. Many species of plants and animals that have become extinct would still exist. Many others that are endangered would be plentiful. The Nature Conservancy (1990) stated that one-fifth of the animals that are now part of our environment will no longer exist by the year 2000 unless we make a conscious effort to preserve them. Young adolescents are particularly sensitive to threats to the environment. The media makes them aware of the problem, and they want to be actively involved in helping with the solution. However, they tend to be naive in their approach to the problem and somewhat simplistic in their proposed solutions. This may be due, at least in part, to a lack of knowledge as to the extent of the problem.

There are many questions that may lead to exploratory topics.

— How can junk mail be stopped?
— What can be done about the plastic six-pack holders that present danger to birds and marine life?
— How can middle school students verify the extent to which the public is aware of phosphate levels in local streams and lakes?
— What will motivate citizens to take action?
— Do special events such as Earth Day make a difference?
— How much water is wasted in the average household?
— What problem is caused by plastics?
— Why use paper sacks, waxed paper, unbleached coffee filters, and reusable food containers?
— What are some alternatives?
— What kinds of conservation are related to water heaters and the electricity required to keep them at 140° Fahrenheit?
— What kinds of house paint create hazardous waste?

— How can paint and paintbrushes be disposed of safely?

— Can old auto tires be recycled?

— What happens when they are placed in a landfill?

— How much energy can be saved by adjusting the thermostat on furnaces and air conditioners?

— How can grocery store shoppers help with conservation?

— What danger is caused by the use of disposable diapers?

— How can paper be recycled?

— How can recycling be required? What is thrown away as garbage — paper, glass, cans, bottles — that can be recycled?

— What can people do in their own yards to create a wildlife refuge?

— What resources are available in your own community for recycling waste? (If such a program exists, the person in charge may be interviewed and asked to answer many of these questions.)

The destruction of the world's rain forests may be the most critical of the attacks on the planet. These tropical rain forests, which receive four to eight meters of rain each year, are located in a narrow region near the Equator in Africa, South and Central America, and in Asia. They are being destroyed so fast that 80% of them may be gone by the year 2000. Why are they being destroyed? Who is responsible? What can be done to save them?

A possibly irreparable hole has been made in the ozone layer, the stratospheric coating that protects us from the damaging ultraviolet rays. What has caused this destruction? How will it affect you and the members of your family? Can it shorten your life? What can be done to repair the hole?

Another man-made dilemma results from the smoke and soot spewed into the environment. The condition caused by this pollution is known as the "greenhouse effect," and it includes global warming that may result in widespread drought, famine, and floods that would be caused by the melting of ice caps. Students may wish to visit a local greenhouse to gain some understanding of the origin of the term. What indications are there that environmental warming is occurring? What may be the consequences?

Still another phenomenon is the El Niño effect, which has brought severe weather changes in the western coastal areas of North America, Central America, and South America. What has caused it? What is the origin of the term? Do scientists relate it to the Christian faith? What can be done to diminish the potential harm?

Local Natural Resources

Every community has its share of natural resources, precious metals, ore, minerals, plants, trees, or some other form. What are these resources where you live? How do they benefit people? What varieties of animal life live in your area? What conditions provide the natural habitat for these animals? What can be done to preserve these animals? What would happen if these animals ceased to exist? What is the official bird of your state? The state flower? tree? How has each of these played a part in the economy of your state? What natural resources contribute most to the economy of your state?

Endangered Species

Some animals will never be seen by people today because they have become extinct. This group includes, of course, the dinosaurs and saber-tooth tigers, but there are many that until recent years roamed certain sections of the planet. What are some of these animals? What species of animals that are common to our country are not found in other countries that have a similar climate? For example, there are many varieties of snakes in the United States, but there are none in Ireland — and there never has been! How would life be different if some of the more common species of animals found in our country were no longer here? What differences would there be if dogs, cats, and gerbils became endangered? How would students' lives be different? What is the difference between "endangered" and "threatened?"

Are there organizations that are attempting to protect endangered and threatened species? How can middle school youngsters determine the knowledge that people in their communities have about endangered and threatened species? What can they do to help to educate the community?

Students can research this topic and design posters, brochures, newspaper articles, and radio and television spot announcements in an attempt to increase public awareness. They may develop a display with pictures and information about some of the threatened species such as the grizzly bear, southern sea otter, prairie dog, and the bald eagle. Another poster or news brief might feature the California condor, bobcat, bison, white-tailed deer, jaguar, and the humpback whale. More than 300 species fit into this category.

With so many living things that share the environment with man in danger of extinction, man himself may also be endangered. Humans, animals, and plants are interdependent. When one species becomes extinct, the delicate balance of nature is altered. Some animals are able to adapt to changes that are thrust upon them by humans. Humans may be the least adaptable. If, as the Nature Conservancy (1990) has said, one-fifth of the animals presently in the world may be extinct by the year 2000, which ones are they likely to be? Will humans be among the survivors?

We may become an endangered species because of our own behavior. We are threatened by an environment we have defiled. We have become addicted to chemicals. We have become lawless in order to support our addictions. We have become endangered by AIDS and other physical illnesses that are largely of our own making. We have moved away from the concept of a nuclear family. Perhaps the human being should be added to the list of endangered species.

Nuclear Power and You

For centuries Americans have burned our natural resources for fuel. These resources include lumber, oil, coal, natural gas and other fossil fuels. We became dependent on these fuels by the machinery we have manufactured — furnaces and internal combustion engines in automobiles, for example.

During World War II nuclear power was released for the first time when the atomic bombs were dropped on the Japanese cities of Hiroshima and Nagasaki. Although many Americans were pleased because nuclear bombs brought the war to an end, there were those who questioned unleashing this weapon on the world. Government officials were quick to assure the people that there would be many peaceful uses for nuclear power. Impetus for the building of nuclear power plants came with the energy crisis of the late 1970s although some plants had been constructed earlier. Accidents at the nuclear power plants at Three Mile Island in Pennsylvania and at Grenoble in the Soviet Union caused the public to express concern about the safety of nuclear energy.

What is nuclear energy? What does it mean to "split the atom?" What is nuclear physics? A nuclear reactor? What is nuclear fission? What are the potential uses of nuclear power? What are the dangers? How does one dispose of nuclear waste? Why do people object to having nuclear waste disposal sites in their states? How is the nuclear power industry regulated? What was the Atomic Energy Commission? What is the Nuclear Regulatory Commission? What is a "nuclear winter?" If a true nuclear winter were to occur, what might be the cause(s)? How would our everyday lives be affected?

Optics and Light

Another common element of our everyday lives is light. Early adolescents may find the study of light to be an interesting pursuit. They may wish to concentrate on physical optics (the genesis, nature, and properties of light), physiological optics (the part light plays in vision), or on geometrical optics (the study of the geometry involved in the reflection and refraction of light as viewed through the study of the mirror and the lens). How fast does light travel? What is a "light year?" What was the contribution of Sir Isaac Newton to the study of optics? What scientific instruments depend on optics? How does the camera use optics? How can mirrors be used to send messages? How is the lens of the camera similar to the lens of the human eye? What is the difference between reflection and refraction? What are concave lens? convex lens? How does a lens work in a microscope? in a telescope? in a camera?

Microbiology

Humans share the environment with many plants and animals. Some of these living things are so small that they can only be seen through the most powerful microscopes. These organisms that co-exist with us may enhance our lives — such as those that cause the pleasant odors enjoyed on a spring day. Some tiny organisms help humans breathe. Still others may cause disease.

What varieties of tiny organisms live in our homes? Sleep in our beds? Sit on our breakfast tables? Sit on our shoulders all day? Which of these tiny organisms are beneficial? Which ones may be harmful? What destroys bacteria? Fungi? What happens when both the beneficial and the harmful bacteria are destroyed? What part do bacteria play in developing foods such as yogurt? What causes "red tide?"

Sound

Although we are surrounded by sound most of our lives, we do not attend to a large percentage of it. We seem to "tune out" those sounds that are part of our everyday experiences. We often ignore repetitive sounds such as that of crickets on a summer night, the ticking of a clock, or the soft humming of a refrigerator. We listen to sirens, bells, and screams. What causes us to pay attention to these sounds and not to others?

Sound is energy. The length of the vibrating body effects sound. The length of a violin, cello, or viola string can be shortened using fingering techniques. Students may want to attempt to vary the pitch of a sound made by a violin string by moving their fingers up and down on a single string. They may use a single string to play a tune.

How does the height of an air column affect sound? Is there a group of musical instruments that rely on air columns to produce sound? How do brass instruments make musical sound? What principle applies to woodwinds? To percussion instruments?

Sometimes sounds may be heard for great distances — such as those heard across a body of water. Solids and liquids conduct sound in different ways. Students may explore these differences.

At times we think we hear a particular sound when that sound is really made artificially. Coconut shells or wood blocks may be used to imitate the sound of horses' hooves. A whistle may sound like a bird. Radio programs include many types of sound effects. There are many instances in television in which sound effects are used. Early adolescents may want to write a radio play (perhaps a ghost story) or a mystery set in their school and record it using their own sound effects. They might also use an audio tape recorder to record only the sound of a television program and analyze the use of sound effects and "mood music."

Students may be fascinated by the Doppler shift, by which the pitch of sound is changed due to the changing proximity of the sound producing instrument to the listener and the speed of sound. They may become more aware of this phenomenon by using a tape recorder to preserve the sound of a monologue when the speaker moves closer and then farther away from the microphone. How is the sound different when it is heard by the human ear and when it is based on a recording? What are the potential uses of the Doppler shift?

Many youngsters like to listen to radios through stereo headsets. It seems that the higher the volume, the more they like it. They may be interested in the experiments that have been done with plants using loud, soft, soothing, and disharmonic music (Ott, 1976). What are the potential effects of such music on the human body? If there physiological danger in attending rock music concerts?

Machines

A logical starting point in exploring machines is with the mechanics of movement. The study of the inclined plane, levers, wheels and axles, cams and cranks, pulleys, screws, drills and augers, rotating wheels, springs, and friction might be topics for an introductory unit. Further study might be focused on harnessing the elements, working with waves (light, sound, photography), and the study of electricity and automation.

Students may find many examples of machines in their homes, at school, and in the neighborhood. Bulletin boards and collages might be constructed to illustrate the different kinds and categories of machines. They might visit an automobile repair or carpentry shop to see the many kinds of tools used by craftsmen whose work is focused on a specific product. They might speculate on some yet to be invented machines that might make people's lives easier and/or more enjoyable. Magazines devoted to mechanics for the home craftsman might be examined to aid in developing such a list.

Coriolis Force

One of the most fascinating natural phenomena that affect all beings is the Coriolis force, or pull. The earth spins as it moves in orbit. At the Equator the speed is toward the east at 1,041 miles per hour. As one travels north (or south) the rate slows. In Florida it moves at 920 miles per hour; in London and Warsaw (which are at the same degrees of latitude) it is moving at 620 miles per hour. At the North Pole the speed is 0 miles per hour. The slippage (or difference in speed) is known as the Coriolis force.

If a giant cannon shell were fired from Miami directly at New York City, it would miss its target by a great distance. The earth would have moved to such a degree that New York City would be much farther east than it was when the cannon was fired. This is because of the Coriolis force. It pulls us sideways with every step and affects bikes, skateboards, automobiles, hurricanes, and torna-does. Because it affects storms, meteorologists have to account for it in tracking them.

The National Aeronautics and Space Administration (NASA) must consider the Coriolis force in launching space vehicles. The location of the Kennedy Space Center at Cape Canaveral, florida was not just because it seemed like a pleasant place to have such an installation. It was selected by scientists after considering many factors, including the Coriolis force.

Great Scientists

The world's greatest scientists (both past and present) may serve as models for young scientists. Many of those who will lead the scientific community and make important scientific breakthroughs in the next century are today's middle school students. How did earlier "greats" become involved in the study of science? At what age? What sacrifices did they make in order to pursue their work?

Students may become acquainted with American scientists such as Thomas Edison, Arthur Compton, and Jonas Salk or with numerous scientists from other countries such as Galileo, Leonardo da Vinci, Einstein, Madame Curie, Mendenhall, and Pasteur. What were the lives of these scientists like during the years they were early adolescents? Did their families support their involvement in scientific work? What obstacles did they overcome in their careers? How did the times in which they lived affect the work they did and the contributions that they made? If those who are no longer alive were somehow brought back to life and were able to work in our country today, what projects would they be likely to work on? Considering the times in which we live, what scientific discoveries are needed to improve the lives of people in our country? In the world?

What rewards are given to scientists? Do they earn large sums of money for their work? Who was Albert Nobel? What did he invent? Is it ironic that he invented something that is incompatible with peace? When was his invention first used? How are recipients of the Nobel prize selected?

Careers in Science

There are many jobs available in science and there are many categories of science. For example, marine science needs oceanographers, biologists, salvage divers, fish culturalists, meteorologists, dredge operators, zoologists, and Coast Guardsmen. Environmental science positions include tree surgeons, landscape architects, geologists, air pollution controllers, wildlife managers, and forest rangers. Still other careers are as biologists, chemists, physicists, and naturalists.

Youngsters may look through the want ads in newspapers and identify jobs that require a knowledge of science. They may speculate as to the types of jobs that may be available in the next decade. Charts, tables, and posters illustrating present and future positions in science may be developed. As is true with so many topics, these activities cut across "content" barriers to provide an integrated approach to the curriculum.

SOCIAL STUDIES

Most social studies teachers view their content specialization area as the major unifying component of the curriculum. Because social studies focuses on the nature of mankind and the world in which we live, social studies is often the central subject for interdisciplinary instruction. The involvement of other subjects areas, of course, is essential, but leadership and initiative in developing interdisciplinary instruction frequently lies with social studies teachers.

A Nation of Immigrants

Many early adolescents may not realize that all Americans have in their family backgrounds persons who immigrated from other countries. This is even true of Native Americans (American Indians), whom anthropologists believe may have come to the North American continent across the Bering Strait from Asia.

Youngsters might begin their study of this topic by interviewing the faculty and staff of their school in order to identify countries from which the ancestors of these adults originated. Countries that are represented could be marked on a map of the world. Students might interview community members in order to determine additional ancestral backgrounds and mark these countries on the map. Colored string or yarn might be used to indicate the place from which the family moved and the state(s) to which the early members of these families immigrated. Many people will have more than one country to report. For countries identified lists of certain characteristics might be prepared covering such items as major language, religious groups, native dishes, famous people from that country, idioms, and everyday words that may have originated in that country. Family life in these countries might also be investigated — including the "rites of passage" into adolescence and adulthood.

Ethnicity

Many different ethnic groups may live in the same country, the same city, and even in the same neighborhood. The difference between "race" and "ethnic group" might be explored. What ethnic groups are represented within the school? How can one learn one's ethnic background? What does it mean to be a member of a specific ethnic group? What physical characteristics identify an ethnic group? What are ethnic foods? Are there any ethnic restaurants in your city? What books, tapes, or other resources does your library have that help to explain life as part of an ethnic group?

Minority Groups

The identification of minority groups is dependent on the identification of the majority group. Everyone who is not part of the majority group is by definition part of the minority. Most of us belong to several minority groups based on our age, sex, physical characteristics, religious affiliations, ethnic background, or other factors. For example, most of the world's population has dark hair and dark eyes. All other people are part of a minority group. Most Americans would probably say that they are Christians. Moslems, Hindus, Jews, and Buddhists represent minority groups in the United States as do atheists and agnostics. Few of us are celebrities. Those who are represent a distinct minority group. A group may represent a majority in one situation and a minority group in another. Most people in your home may be males while most of the people in your class are females. What minority groups are represented in your city? In your school? To what minority groups do you belong?

Civil Liberties

As Americans we live in a country in which the rights of every individual are protected by the U.S. Constitution. The rights of members of minority groups are as important as those of the majority. Youngsters may identify legislation that guarantees protection of civil rights. What rights are covered by the Bill of Rights? Why are such laws necessary? Are the civil rights of citizens of most other countries protected to the extent that we are protected in our country? What organizations have been established to oversee the enforcement of civil rights? Do the civil rights of some groups infringe on the civil rights of other groups? What is done when this happens? How is the guarantee of separation of church and state in the U.S. Constitution related to civil liberties? How does this constitutional amendment relate to prayer in schools? To Christmas pageants? Should church property be taxed? What types of courts have jurisdiction over cases involving violation of civil rights? What might happen to someone who violates your civil rights?

Freedom of speech is protected by the Constitution. Is this a *total* freedom? Should all views be heard? The right to privacy is also protected by the U.S. Constitution. How might this right be violated by mandatory drug testing? By mandatory testing for AIDS?

You and the Law

People who live together in groups must have laws in order to protect everyone's rights. There are different types of laws with different types of jurisdictions. What is case law? What is statutory law? Most federal laws are based on an interpretation of the Constitution and/or are established by Congress. State laws are passed by state legislative bodies. All laws must be constitutional — that is, they must not violate the rights that are guaranteed by the U.S. Constitution. There are many laws that are common across the entire United States. For example, in all states the killing of another human being is considered a homicide and is against the law. In all states stealing is considered a violation of the law. All states have a legal speed limit for automobiles. However, there is great variation among the states as to laws regarding elections, automobile exhaust emissions, the age at which a person is considered to be an adult, etc. Why do some states have personal income tax while others do not? Does your state have this kind of tax? Should this be the same in all states? There is even greater variation in laws among cities. In many cities there are still laws in effect that may be completely irrelevant in modern times. Such laws may deal with the hitching of horses on major thoroughfares or the regulation about hanging one's laundry out to dry on certain days of the week. Middle school students might interview city officials in order to identify some of these outmoded laws. Local state legislators may be asked how state laws are passed. How are laws repealed?

Crime and Criminals

Unless an early adolescent has a law enforcement officer or an attorney in the family, most of what the individual knows about crime and criminals is probably based on television programs or movies. Pursuit of the following questions and activities will broaden that knowledge.

What is a crime? What's the difference between a civil and a criminal court case? What is a felony? A misdemeanor? What does it mean to have committed a capital crime? What types of courts hear criminal cases? Civil cases? How is a lawsuit handled? Can someone other than a lawyer defend someone in court?

If you were arrested for committing a crime, what are your rights? What does it mean to "post bond?" What is the age limit under which an individual can be tried as a juvenile defendant? How are juries selected? Can anyone be called to serve on a jury? Who is a defense attorney? A public defender? A prosecutor? A bailiff? What type of educational preparation must an attorney have? How do judges get their jobs? Can a defendant be tried twice for the same identical crime? What does the term "double jeopardy" mean? Is everyone who commits a crime considered a criminal? What kinds of sentences can be imposed on people convicted of a crime? Who decides what the sentence will be?

Ethics

Middle school students now hear more and more about governmental ethics. The incident that became known as "Watergate" made most Americans aware that government officials are not always honest or right. What is meant by a code of ethics? What is included in such a code? Can something that is legal be unethical? Is a man who steals bread to feed his starving family committing an illegal or an unethical act? Do people who obey the law because they are afraid of being punished act ethically? What is meant by "situational ethics?" Is having a code of ethics required if an occupational group is to be considered a profession? What groups can the student identify that have developed their own codes of ethics? What are the elements of these codes? Students may wish to write their own personal codes of ethics or one for the class.

Censorship

What does the term "censorship" mean? What is the origin of the word "censor?" Why should any person or any group want to censor materials in a library or media center? What groups have attempted to remove these materials? Has any group in your city attempted to censor materials? What was the basis for their actions? What are some of the groups that have fought against censorship? What have they used as the basis for their objections? How does the First Amendment to the Constitution relate to censorship? Should there be limits to free speech? Should print and electronic news media be regulated? Should the content be checked by someone or some group? What is the Freedom of Information Act? Whose values should prevail? The majority group? Certain minorities? Both? Religious conservatives? Radical fringe groups?

What is pornography? Should pornographic materials be censored? Who should decide if something is pornographic? What is "kiddie porn?" Have other nations and cultures experienced controversy related to censorship? What has the U.S. Supreme Court ruled about censorship? The state courts?

Science and Religion

Since the earliest of times people have sought a supreme being to explain the origin and reasons for the existence of the universe. Ancient Egyptians worshipped a sun god; the ancient Greeks were not content to worship only one God, they had a variety of gods and goddesses who specialized in certain areas of life such as love, war, speed, and beauty. A super god, Zeus, and his goddess wife, Hera, ruled all of the others. The Romans liked the Greek gods so much that they gave them Roman names and adopted them as their own. They assigned the same areas of specialization to these gods and goddesses as had the Greeks. Norse gods were fewer in number but no less spectacular in their deeds than those of the Greeks and Romans. Often these gods were used to explain phenomena that modern man would understand to be perfectly natural — such as the changing of the seasons, the eruption of volcanoes, or the reason for ferocious storms.

Religious groups have attempted to explain the origin of the universe. Scientists have offered alternative explanations of the event. What is one scientific explanation? What is meant by the "big bang?" How do various religious groups explain the origin of the universe? Is there conflict between certain religious and some scientific explanations of other events? What sources are available that might help one to find "the truth?" Might there be instances in which both the scientific and the religious explanations of events may both be correct?

Extremist Groups

Almost every day there are reports in the media about extremist groups. What is an extremist group? Is any group that goes to "extremes" to further a cause an "extremist group?" An extremist group (Barnette, 1972) is made up of people who are excessive in their views and in their actions. Some of these groups are often called "fanatics" by people who are in the political majority. These groups have been known to act as if they are not required to obey laws with which they do not agree or that they feel are unjust. Often they react in response to threats — either real or imagined. Extremist groups may be racial, political, social, or religious.

Groups may be labelled as at the "extreme left" because they distrust the Establishment (U.S. political majority) or they may be referred to as the "extreme right" because they draw their membership from those who overreact to a real or perceived threat from others such as that of other racial or ethnic groups or from a political group's "secret agents" inside the United States.

Extremist groups may share many of the same characteristics whether they are from the "left" or from the "right." For example they: distrust the democratic process and the court system, oversimplify complex social problems, label any opposition as part of an organized conspiracy, distrust governmental or private attempts at international cooperation, view "the cause" as more important than the people in the organization, and, refuse to see other people's viewpoints if these differ from their own.

Students who explore the topic of extremist groups might identify groups such as: Student Nonviolent Coordinating Committee (SNCC), Weathermen, Black Panther Party, Youth International Party (the "Yippies"), John Birch Society, Ku Klux Klan, National Socialist White People's Party (formerly the American Nazi Party), Minutemen, and the Aryan Nation. In what ways are these groups similar? Why do people form extremist groups? Could extremist groups exist in societies that are not democratic? Do extremist groups play on people's fears? What tactics are used by extremist groups? Find some examples of these tactics such as: creating hysteria and fear, coercing and intimidating those who dissent, developing propaganda outlets, or appealing for money to fight the enemy.

Why do Americans need to know about extremist groups? What can citizens do to combat the work of extremists?

Terrorism

What is terrorism? Terrorist groups act with or threaten to commit violent acts in order to frighten their opponents or make public grievances that may be real or imaginary. These acts of violence may include bombings, kidnappings, airplane or ship hijacking, the taking of hostages, or murder. The term probably originated during the French Revolution with a period known as the Reign of Terror (1793-94). The meaning of the term "terrorism" has taken on new meaning in the twentieth century — especially since World War II. The dictators Hitler, Mussolini, and Stalin used political terrorism to rise to power. Certain groups have used terrorism (often against innocent civilians) in an attempt to gain the release of criminals and to make other political demands.

Students may seek answers to many questions. Are terrorist groups also extremist groups? Are all extremist groups also terrorists? Are there religious terrorist groups? Are there terrorist groups presently at work in our own country? Why do some terrorist groups such as the Ku Klux Klan wear certain types of clothing during their activities? Why does the Klan burn crosses at its meetings? Why are crosses sometimes burned on people's lawns? How and where did the Ku Klux Klan begin? What reason was given for its establishment? Can white, Protestant, Anglo-Saxon women and children hold full membership in the KKK? What ethnic, racial, and religious groups does the Klan oppose? What acts of violence has the Klan committed? What is the Aryan Nation? What do members claim to be its purposes? What groups does this group oppose? Does the group wear certain types of clothing to distinguish it from the average citizen?

What is the Palestine Liberation Organization? The Red Brigade? The Irish Republican Army? What are the purposes of these organizations? What acts of violence have they committed? What groups of people do these terrorist groups consider their enemies?

What are some examples of terrorist activities during the last ten years? Are there organizations that are openly opposed to terrorist groups? What can the average American citizen do to combat terrorism? Students may review old newspapers and news magazines in order to identify reports of terrorism.

Death and Dying

All organisms die, but humans are probably the only beings that are aware that they will die. Many middle school youngsters will have experienced the death of a pet or that of an older member of their family. What does it mean to be dead?

Why are bodies examined in a post-mortem examination? What does "post mortem" mean? Is an autopsy performed on the body of every person who dies? Does the dead person's family have to request an autopsy before one will be performed? What training does a coroner or medical examiner need?

How many different legal means are there for the disposition of a dead body? What is the most often used method? Does a person have to own a cemetery lot in order to be buried? Under what circumstances would a body that has been interred (buried) likely be exhumed? What legal process must take place before a grave is opened? What is cremation? Why do some people request that their bodies be cremated? What is done with the person's ashes? What is the Poseidon Society?

What does a mortician do to a dead body in preparing it for burial? What does he/she do to prepare a body for cremation? Does the law in your state require that bodies be embalmed? What group of ancient people were noted for the preservation of the bodies of the dead? What kind of training does a mortician need?

Old people are not the only ones who die. Sometimes middle school age youngsters die. What are the five leading causes of death among early adolescents? What are the leading causes of death in the general population?

Some people develop deadly diseases and know they will die long before they succumb. Elizabeth Kubler-Ross (1987) suggested that there are five emotional phases that people go through from the time they are diagnosed as having a fatal illness until their deaths. These are: denial and isolation, anger, bargaining, depression, and acceptance. How might a person behave in each of these stages? People who know they are going to die need people who are willing to be supportive during the last years, months, weeks, or days of their lives. What is hospice? Does your community have a hospice organization? Are there hospice services in your local hospital(s)? Does it require special preparation for a health worker to take care of a terminally ill patient?

What is a will? What are the laws of your state concerning wills? What is a "living will?" Can a will be drawn up by someone other than an attorney? Must it be written? What happens if a person dies and doesn't have a will? How old should people be before they need a will? If you were to drawn up a will at this time, who would you want to have your possessions? Students might interview their adult friends and families to determine how knowledgeable they may be about wills.

Local Legends and Heroes

Most cities, towns, and villages have some kind of local legend. The legend may relate to some historical event and may include some degree of fact. Take, for example, the legend of Robin Hood. There really was a person who was Robin of Locksley. His motives and his deeds may not have been exactly as they were portrayed in literature and in films. As the legend has been told by each generation, the reputation of the hero and the deeds attributed to him and his merry men may have been grossly exaggerated.

Local legends may involve athletes, law-enforcement officers, war heroes, entertainers, or some other special persons. Usually a legend is based on an event or a series of events that go beyond what would ordinarily be expected in the lives of most people. Heroes are often ordinary people who find themselves in extraordinary situations. The story of SGT Alvin York and his capture of an enormous number of German soldiers during one battle in World War I is but one example.

Youngsters may obtain a history of their areas in order to determine legends that may persist. Interviewing elderly citizens, members of the local historical society, or city officials may yield many such legends.

Newspaper and magazine articles as well as radio and television news bits provide a rich basis for local legends and make for the identification of local heroes. Students may develop their own legends from these news releases. They might even fantasize about themselves as performing some heroic act.

U.S. and State Parks and Recreation Areas

Most states have parks — land and facilities set aside for the use of the public. President Theodore Roosevelt (for whom the Teddy Bear was named) is given credit for his vision in purchasing land for national parks. President Franklin Roosevelt is given credit for bringing the parks and facilities to optimal usage level. If it were not for these two presidents, Americans and visitors from other countries would not be able to enjoy Yellowstone, Yosemite, or the Great Smoky Mountains National Parks. What agency of the federal government supervises national parks? What dangers do national parks face in the next twenty years? What proportion of federally-owned land is set aside for parks? How does this compare with the proportions in 1980? 1960? 1940? Why should this land be protected? Is the federal government acquiring more land for parks?

State parks are on land that is owned by the state. Some of these parks provide facilities for camping, picnicking, boating, swimming, and fishing; others are left in a somewhat "natural" condition. Where are the state parks in your state? What facilities are available at the state park nearest your home? Students might interview a park ranger about the history of the park, facilities available, wildlife and vegetation that live there, and the problems of maintaining the park. Is your state setting aside additional parcels of land for parks?

Community Service

Americans always seem to want to help those less fortunate than themselves — the "underdogs." Middle school students have a keen sense of justice. They genuinely care about the poor, the sick, the hungry, the homeless, and the elderly. Many students may be interested in reading to the blind, to young children in day care centers, and to residents in hospitals and nursing homes. They may wish to adopt one of these centers, visit them, and write letters to or for the residents.

They may be interested in tutoring other students. Even a poor reader in grade six can work effectively with students in grade one. Results of research support the notion that the tutor may benefit as much (or more) from peer tutoring as does the tutee.

Middle school students have become aware that the environment is endangered. Many communities have formed organizations and developed programs that are directed toward the protection of the environment. These groups may be open to the establishment of youth auxiliaries.

Personal Finance

Most early adolescents are interested in receiving money of their own either through gifts from family or friends or by earning it. They have difficulty with long-term savings plans, however. Youngsters may determine a short-range goal, determine a means of acquiring money, develop a written budget for necessities, and determine a savings plan.

Some youngsters may plan to mow lawns, or shovel snow (depending on the season and the climate), deliver newspapers, or babysit. How can the public be informed that a youngster is available for this type of work? What will make the youngster and his/her services attractive to clients? What marketing skills are used by those who sell their services? Middle schoolers may want to interview service professionals such as television repair specialists, attorneys, medical professionals, and others. A visit to a local supermarket or restaurant might enable youngsters to see several types of business cards that are displayed on a bulletin board. An evening spent monitoring television commercials might reveal not only the number of ads for businesses that are service oriented but advertising techniques that are used by the company.

Students might prepare their own advertising posters using computer graphics and may write radio spot announcements or fliers, or even business cards.

Controversial Issues

These issues differ according to location and the times in which one seeks to identify them. A topic that may be controversial today may not be tomorrow. The Connecticut Education Association and the Council on Interracial Books for Children (1981) offer the following caution for teachers ". . . productive discussion of a controversial issue can take place only in a classroom in which the atmosphere is open and accepting. Respect for the ideas of others and appreciation of differences should be openly expressed and consistently practiced" (p. 9). A wise teacher will be able to determine those issues that are appropriate and those that are not.

Some controversial issues are perennial. Some others are of recent origin. Students may attempt to identify both types of issues through news reports and/ or interviews. Teachers may suggest possible issues. Students should be reminded that there are *at least* two points of view in every issue. In order to be fair all sides should be investigated and reported. It is not necessary that students arrive at any conclusion as to the side of the issue they espouse.

Careers in Social Studies

There are many careers for which a knowledge of social studies is important. However, it shouldn't be assumed that mere knowledge of history, geography, economics, sociology, anthropology, psychology, and political science are in and of themselves all that is necessary for success in one of these careers. A well-prepared person who engages in any of these occupations must have skills and knowledge in other curriculum areas.

Among those careers that require a background in social studies are: lawyers, police officers, cartographers, fire fighters, park rangers, politicians, historians, economists, sociologists, teachers, and psychologists. Students may interview people who have pursued these occupations in an attempt to determine more specifically what knowledge of social studies was useful to them.

CHAPTER FOUR
Exploration Through Special Content Areas

The most traditional designation of the exploratory portion of the curriculum includes courses in art, music, physical education, health, home living, industrial arts, and the information sciences. All too often such exploratory areas have been assigned a second-class status as if they weren't really as important as language arts, social studies, math, and science. This has been manifested in categories on report cards and other types of documents. Often the "content areas" are listed first with the "others" listed separately. Sometimes the grading system is different for these special content areas.

Educators who know and understand early adolescents recognize the importance of these "special content" areas. These professionals believe that they are equal in importance.

This section is presented not only for teachers of these courses but for all middle school teachers so that they may recognize the interweaving of all content — that it can never truly be separated. Teachers in all areas have an obligation to identify ways of integrating content so that students may recognize the relationships that exist. For the purpose of presentation only, the "special content" areas are discussed separately.

MUSIC

Gardner (1983) has defined seven different kinds of intelligence. Among these he describes musical intelligence as being separate and unique. Unfortunately, in our schools we consider music as less important than linguistic and logical mathematical intelligence. If music is offered it is usually in the form of band or chorus. These two offerings, while important, are not substitutes for an effective and well-planned course in music that would be taken by all pupils and would be geared to understanding and appreciating music rather than performing. Band is available only to those who can afford an instrument and a limited number for whom the school can furnish an instrument. Chorus is for those males whose voices have changed and a very few who don't mind being sopranos or altos. These two activities cannot satisfy the need for an exploratory course in music. Middle grades are the last chance for almost all students to attain musical literacy.

Music is an important part of our heritage and our everyday lives. It is through our music that we tell the rest of the world about who we are as a nation. Everyone should have the opportunity to become acquainted with the music that defines our contemporary lives and attitudes. They should also have the opportunity to become acquainted with music from around the world. Some activities that are likely to get middle grade students excited about music are presented in the sections below.

Music Is Interesting

Adler and McCarroll (1981) list several ways teachers can plan a music class that will turn them on every day. Start with music they enjoy, what they listen to on the radio or television. There is even music in elevators and dentists' offices. We are surrounded by music. Find out which music students enjoy and start with that music. Let students talk while they listen to music. At times encourage them to draw while music is playing, read while music is playing, and even do their homework to music. They can dance to music, do eurythmics or aerobics, or just walk while music is playing. They can learn about music that tells a story. Middle level students appreciate a song like "Why Can't a Woman Be More Like a Man" from Lerner and Loewe's *My Fair Lady*. The story of *Pygmalion* is very simple and the part this song plays in the musical is easy to get across to students. Middle grades students can relate immediately to the "girl hating" that this song describes.

Keep musical terms simple. Musical language can become very esoteric, but it does not need to be. Teachers should frequently surprise students with something in music. For instance, on an ethnic holiday play some ethnic music. On a composer's birthday, music composed by that composer would be an appropriate surprise. Classical music is important. Start with light classics and give information about the composition or the composer that will be interesting or humorous. If possible start with major works that contain humor, such as Mozart's *The Magic Flute*. In the story Papageno lies and claims he has killed a serpent that was chasing him. As punishment for lying, three attendants of the queen, who really killed the serpent, place a padlock on his mouth. It becomes humorous as he tries to speak.

Music Is Diverse

Music has power over our lives. People use music to relax. They sleep to music, meditate with music, and dream fantastic dreams to the strains of music. A band rendering a football spirit song can get an entire stadium excited. Music heightens suspense and emotion in movies and television programs. Even before we had sound in movies, pianists were hired to improvise music to accompany the action on the screen. Music is an important part of a church service. A broad range of music has been written to enrich worship in the church from Bach's Chorales to gospel music like Mahalia Jackson's singing "He's Got the Whole World in His Hands." Music has been written to paint mental images. It is not difficult to sense the ebb and flow of water in Mendelssohn's "Fingal's Cave." The sensations people experience with Ravel's "Bolero" vary with the experiences of the listener. Music is used to describe love repeatedly from country music to contemporary popular music and to operatic arias. Music is used as therapy with mentally disturbed persons.

There is music from Broadway and grand opera. There is ballet music and popular dance music. Different cultures are expressed in their dance music. A mazurka, a waltz, a rhumba, a samba, tango, a Virginia Reel, or a hula dance all are associated with a particular culture. Different religious music is associated with very different religious services. Jazz is the kind of music that is associated with the United States more than any other kind of music. Various kinds of ethnic music are associated with many different ethnic groups that live throughout our country. There is vocal music that speaks a message through the words as they are sung to appropriate melodies. There is instrumental music that speaks a message that is less explicit and more dependent on the listener to complete. Understanding the diversity in music is part of becoming musically literate. There is no question but that music has power and influence over our lives every day. Middle grade students can not only enjoy studying the many ways music affects each of us, they will gain important understandings.

Songs About Cities, States, and Nations

Many songs have been written about different cities and states. They can take a trip on the "Chattanooga Choo Choo" and trace their trip on a map. Middle grade students will add to your list of songs which could include: "Meet Me in St. Louis, Louis," "I Left My Heart in San Francisco," "Nothing Could Be Finer Than to Be in Carolina in the Morning," "Back Home in Indiana," "Stars Fell on Alabama," "Georgia on My Mind," "Missouri Waltz," and "Tennessee Waltz." What are the stories behind these songs?

No song touches our emotions more than the national anthem. All Americans should attend the flag raising ceremony at the Parris Island Marine Corps Station in order to feel for themselves the full meaning of our nation, flag, and national anthem. Sometimes national anthems of other nations bring tears to our eyes. "La Marseillaise" moves many people other than the French. It has a rich national heritage to support it. "O Canada" is a particularly beautiful anthem that reminds us that we are particularly close to Canada in many ways.

Musical Drama

Telling stories through music is as exciting as oral tradition is in telling prose and poetry. We tell stories in music on Broadway or in opera. A Broadway musical such as "Oklahoma," which was popular when the authors were young, has a great American story and great American music to support it. It introduces Rodgers and Hammerstein in one of their finest musicals and brings many singable songs into the music class. The humor of "Poor Jud Is Dead" interests middle grade students. They could build a coffin and sit around on it as they learn to sing this song. They will enjoy many other songs in "Oklahoma" like "Oh, What a Beautiful Morning." They could even move as they sing this song. They won't revolutionize choreography as Agnes De Mille did but they can get into the spirit of this music. Middle grade students can come to appreciate the genius of Rodgers and Hammerstein and the music they wrote.

From Broadway musicals to grand opera is a logical next step. Many operas have stories to tell that are interesting to middle grade students. Verdi was commissioned to write *Aida* to celebrate the opening of the Suez Canal. The story of Radames, an Egyptian warrior, and his love of Aida, an Ethiopian princess, has all the elements that are exciting for preadolescents. The Egyptian Princess Ammeris is jealous of their love. Aida is spying to obtain military information for her father. The opera tells of her inner conflict between her love of her father and Ethiopia and her love for Radames. After Radames wins a victory over Ethiopia, Ammeris sentences Radames, and Aida to be buried alive. It's the kind of story that middle grade students could enjoy even if there were no music. But with music there is an added dimension to the power of the drama. Early adolescents can get excited over opera.

Movement in Music

Music is composed of three elements: melody, harmony, and rhythm. The most important part is usually considered to be rhythm. John Philip Sousa called the drum the king of instruments simply because it dealt only with rhythm. To appreciate music students must be allowed to feel the movement in music and to move with music. Students should clap to some music like "Good News the Chariot's Coming." With a march like Sousa's "Semper Fidelis" students should be encouraged to get up and march. And then there is music that should be danced to enjoy. A good dance for middle grade students is the lively square dance. There are other dances associated with the United States that bring enjoyment to youngsters including the Bunny Hop, Alley Cat, Hokey Pokey, and the Twist. An older dance associated with the United States is the Charleston.

After introducing students to our own dances teachers could open them up to other dances like the waltz and others that are peculiar to different countries. To what sections of the world do they associate the polka, rhumba, tango, or the samba? The tarantella has an interesting story about its origin several centuries ago. In Italy people believed that the only cure for the bite of the tarantula was to dance to the point of exhaustion. Music was written for the tarantella and used for weddings and festive occasions. The hora is a Jewish dance also used at weddings and at times to express happiness. The hora was presented in the Broadway production *Fiddler on the Roof* during a wedding scene. Middle grade students like to dance after they learn how to dance. It is a way of expressing rhythm in music. Dancing cannot be taught hurriedly. It is a gradual process showing how we feel about music.

Building Instruments

Students can build instruments to discover how to create a tone and make it move. Bamboo can be used to create a functional flute. Students can learn how the length of the column of air in the flute can be changed to create the desired tone. As they explore with their instruments they can discover some things about octaves and other things related to overtones.

Stringed instruments, such as a simple dulcimer, can be built by students. As they play their dulcimers students will discover that the length and size of the string determine the frequency of the tone they can develop. When the string is divided in half the octave is created. Students will be able to find out many things about the physics of sound that they would not otherwise have known.

From these beginnings students can be introduced to all the instruments that comprise bands and orchestras. They can learn how to produce a tone on any instrument and how to make that tone move to other tones. They can experience the joy of making a musical tone.

Finally, students can be introduced to the world of percussion instruments and how they are played. Students are quite often surprised at the difficulty in playing a percussion instrument. Middle grade students can begin to feel the intricate rhythms that make music what it is.

Composition

Music gives all of us the opportunity to say something that lies within us but that words cannot express. Middle grade youngsters have much within them that they can't express adequately. With a little help with musical notation students can explore deep within themselves for thought, ideas, and feelings they would like to share with others. In the history of musical composition music was communicated orally even after musical notation had developed to a great deal of precision. Even today there are groups of people who compose with relative freedom relying on the ear alone. Students should be encouraged to compose matching words with music or simply creating melodies they like. Mozarts,

Medelssohns, and Schuberts don't emerge often, but students need to be encouraged in every way possible to explore who they are and what they feel. Perhaps music, if given an opportunity, will help.

Careers in Music

Careers in music may be found in performing, conducting, and educating. In performing music there are careers in symphony orchestras or in night club bands. Musical performers require several years of instruction and deep commitment to performing as a career. Musicians don't typically emerge at the top of their profession overnight. Symphony orchestras depend on a group of people who keep themselves at their peak of performance. Night club performers must keep up to date on their repertoire or they too will be replaced by someone else. There are also pianists and organists who perform, usually on a part-time basis, in churches.

Because public school performing bands and orchestras have very active programs, directors are needed in relatively large numbers. Band directors will need to complete a college program as a music education major. Larger churches hire ministers of music. Smaller churches have directors of music who direct the chancel choirs, youth choirs, and children's choirs. There are many piano teachers who teach students in their own homes. Beyond these careers there are a few people who compose musical scores for television, movies, and Broadway musicals.

The best outcome of an exploratory segment in music is not its likely influence on a career but rather in helping persons tap their musical intelligence and become musically literate. Such persons select music to surround themselves and play in a group for their own pleasure. Music is part of enjoying life, part of a worship experience, and a way of expressing one's emotions.

ART

When students leave the middle school, with limited exceptions, they will have completed whatever art education they will have. Their experiences in high school will most likely side-step any further study of art. *America 2000* is a federal strategy to achieve six very ambitious goals by the beginning of the 21st century. Regretably, these goals do not include art. Instead, there is talk of a "New Generation of American Schools" to enable students to "achieve a quantum leap in learning and to help make America all that it should be" (Governor's Conference, 1991). A curriculum that does not include fine arts will not make America all that it should be.

Art is a basic subject and it should be a part of every middle level student's program. Lipsitz (1984) describes the Shoreham-Wading Middle School as having an art program that "pervades the life of the school surrounding townships." Students need experiences in drawing and painting with different art media. They need to be able to depict visually their ideas, their feelings of elation and depression in art. They need to be able to relate different art to different cultures, different values, and different ways to portray the world around them. However, "art programs suffer in times of anemic budgets" (Messick & Reynolds, 1992).

In this section activities are presented which are designed to coordinate art with the academic part of the curriculum and to enable students to explore the vast arena of art. Some of these activities could be accomplished by teachers with no art specialization but most of them would be considered a part of an exploratory art program. Several of these activities were suggested by Hubbard and Rouse (1977).

Decorative Art

Every classroom needs to be alive, a place where students have their being. Too often schools are drab places that don't reflect the beauty and exuberance of 10 to 14 year olds. Young people could accept the challenge of making the school theirs by exploring ways to decorate classrooms and corridors. There could be drawings and paintings, novel bulletin boards, and living things. Some decorations would be in place for a year or more, while others would be transient and change periodically. Each teacher, working with the classs, could allow students to explore ways they could express themselves artistically.

In appreciating these decorative expressions it must be remembered that expressing one's likes and dislikes or tastes must be distinguished from judging the merit of these artistic expressions. There is no simple philosophical view that can be formulated to cover all of the values that can be expressed. It remains an avenue of exploratory expression that could bring beauty into the decor of the school and bring students to a better understanding of themselves.

Community Resources

If the school is located in an urban area there is a good chance a museum of art is available. The school could arrange to have docents or musum staff visit the school with slides and prints which could introduce the students to what is available in their own community. A field trip to a museum could allow middle level learners to begin an exploration of their own values or the values of cultures and artists throughout the ages. Work of local artists are often on exhibition and the artists could share with students what they have accomplished.

After an introduction to the museum, students should be allowed to explore whatever is in the museum following agreed upon rules. Students should have the opportunity to discover what in art is appealing and of value to them. If they lived in France and visited the Louvre they might find themselves gazing at the *Mona Lisa* and linking to the early 16th century a time that had never been experienced before then.

Incorporating Art into Academic Subjects

Art could be incorporated into most topics presented in the academic subjects. Messick and Reynolds (1992) describe a way of coordinating art with a social studies topic such as colonial or pioneer life. We read of the self-sufficiency of early Americans during these two periods of our history but seldom do people experience the extent of this self-sufficiency. In this activity students could use a comb or brush to card wool and disentangle fibers of the wool. Next the students could spin the yarn and dye it the colors they wanted. The yarn could then be woven into a fabric or knitted.

In planning this activity there would need to be a close working relationship between the art teacher and the interdisciplinary team. As the activity is carried out the students would begin to understand the way colonists and pioneers felt about their lives. They would likely get a sense of a different kind of beauty than they had previously experienced.

Printmaking

One-time print making, called monoprints, was once the simplest kind of printing. Every one is a creative original. Students begin by spreading a layer of thick paint or printer's ink on a flat surface. This surface can be a flat dinner plate made of metal or thick, hard plastic or even shiny pages from a magazines. Then they spread the ink out with a brush or roll it with a brayer, a printer's roller. Next they draw designs in the wet paint or ink using a stick, their fingers, or anything that will make markings in the thin surface. The students will place a piece of paper on the drawing and rub the paper gently with their hands, carefully lifting the paper from the design and hanging it up to dry. Students can then spread another thin layer of paint or ink on the surface and repeat the process, making other monoprints.

There are many objects around us that can be used in printmaking. These objects can be man-made such as nuts, paper clips, or keys. Nature also provides leaves, small twigs, or a corn cob. In this activity, students can practice putting just the right amount of paint or ink on the object and pressing the painted part on a piece of paper. They should fill the entire piece of paper with prints forming a design or creating a picture from their prints. Upon completion they can search for meaning in their printing.

In another printing activity students can make their own gift wrapping paper. They start this activity by gluing a piece of string, which has been formed in some kind of design, onto a piece of cardboard. After the glue is dry, students can paint the string or roll color over it with a brayer. On a large sheet of white paper they can print some design they have discovered by practicing different designs. They can use different colors in their design to create more interest.

In another printing activity, a "block" is made from a potato, carrot, or turnip. Students cut across the root to make a flat surface. Using a small knife they can then cut a simple design in the root to form a printing block. This design should be fairly deep so that the ink or paint is rolled only on the design. Lightly pencilled guidelines can be drawn on the paper to help make the pattern have a uniform appearance.

Interesting designs can be made by using their names. The letters should be approximately $1\frac{1}{2}$" high and $\frac{3}{4}$" wide. The design for their names should be drawn on a piece of linoleum. Students will cut away all the parts of linoleum around the letters of their name. Use a brayer to roll ink on the linoleum and press it firmly onto a piece of paper. Their name will be printed in a mirror image. They can draw this backward print on another piece of linoleum and cut it out as they did the first piece. This will print their name correctly. Students can make an interesting design using both images of their name.

In doing any or all of these activities on printing students will discover many things about printing they had not recognized before. They can also experiment making interesting monograms from the initials of their name. Creative ways of arranging their initials enhances their personal image.

Sculpture

Students who want to do sculpting first need to learn to enjoy the messy feel of mud or clay squeezing between their fingers. If they enjoy this feeling they are well on the way to sculpturing. In an introductory activity, mix a large handful of Plaster of Paris thick enough that it doesn't drip. The students hold it in both hands with their fingers spread apart and squeeze the plaster until it begins to ooze between their fingers. They should not move their fingers until the plaster is quite hard. As the plaster sets it will become quite warm. After the plaster is dry and set they can gently remove their hands.

Another good sculpting material is clay. One way to use clay is to roll it out into 1/4" rope and cut it around to make interesting shapes. One shape would be a clay pot built on a round flat bottom. As the clay rope is coiled around on top of the bottom it can be cemented together by brushing where it touches itself with slip, a creamy mixture of clay and water. After the pot is dry students can leave it as a clay pot or, if there is a kiln in the school, fire it and make it pottery. After this activity, students can make other pots with clay by shaping or pinching with the hands or by fastening slabs of clay together with slip.

Sculptures can be made from things people throw away. This kind of sculpture is called assemblage. The students can collect things made of plastic, glass, wood, or metal, broken or not. These things would normally be thrown away but can be unified as an assemblage. Students join the parts solidly — cuting away parts, opening them up to show what is inside, or leaving them solid. The finished sculpture should be unified from every angle it is viewed.

Another way to produce sculpture is by carving rather than by shaping material or putting pieces together. In the beginning students should use soap or wax. These materials can be carved easily. There is one precaution about carving, be careful about cutting too much at one time. It is much easier to cut away a little bit more than it is to add anything.

Feelings with Colors

Different colors are associated with different feelings. Blue is the color of water, sky, night, and shadows.It can make you feel cool, peaceful, and sad depending on the shade. Red, orange, and purple are colors that are associated with fire, anger, war, fall leaves, and sunset. Green can make you think of Spring or deep shadows in the jungle depending on whether the green is light or dark. Students can choose their favorite color and identify the feelings it elicits.

One activity that associates different colors with different kinds of music is popular with middle grade learners. They can collect pieces of paper in several different colors and textures and several musical tapes representing classical, rock, movie theme tunes, and country music. Let students select music they like. While the music is being played instruct them to make a picture out of the colored paper. They can cut or tear pieces of the paper choosing the color and forming a picture on a sheet of paper that shows how the music makes them feel. When the collage has been completed students may identify the picture by the title of the music.

For bright colors students can explore with tissue paper. These colors become brighter when they are painted with white glue mixed with water. They can look still brighter when they are placed next to some dark construction paper which is usually dull by contrast. Students can crumple tissue paper before gluing it for other effects. Students should explore making their pictures by overlapping with different colors. If they don't like a section of their picture they can cover it with white paper and do it again. When their collage is complete they can highlight certain sections of their picture with black waterproof ink.

Nature produces many beautiful things in color such as feathers, petals on a flower, or scales on a fish. Students can collect some of these things around their homes or schools. They can be arranged in interesting designs to show the different colors. New shapes can be created that show off these natural collections in exciting ways.

To explore with colors students can use crayons and tempera paints. To start this activity they can fill a piece of paper with different shapes and several different colors of crayon. They then cover the entire sheet with thick black tempera paint. After the paint has dried they can draw a picture by etching with a piece of wire or a nail file. The colors underneath will show through. By leaving some of the picture black at some places and letting a lot of color show in other places a very interesting picture can be produced. This crayon etching makes excellent use of different colors and allows students to explore extensively.

Impressionists began painting pictures that cameras could not capture after cameras were invented. They noticed that sunshine had many different colors with very little black or gray in it. They also noticed that as the sun moved the colors changed. There are many impressionists like Pierre Renoir, Claude Monet, and Alfred Sisles who created this kind of painting. Students can be introduced to impressionistic art by drawing a picture very quickly outdoors. It can be any subject but should be drawn quickly so that they can capture the colors in the sunlight.

Henri Matisse painted with many bright colors and very little shadow because shadows made colors dull. Students who like bright colors should look at several paintings of Matisse and then try to use bright colors and very few shadows in their painting.

Finally, students can explore with colored light and colored paper to create effects in color. For centuries there have been stained glass windows in churches. The sunlight coming through stained glass windows makes the interior of a building beautiful in a distinct way. Beauty is drawn directly from the colors in the light. Students can simulate a stained glass window by using thin black cardboard and different colored cellophane. They would start out by drawing a design to fit their window and decide which colors to use in the different sections of the design. After they have colored the design with crayon or paint they can draw the same design on a piece of thin black cardboard and cut out the spaces that are to be colored. Following the drawing they can cement the right color of cellophane on the cardboard.

These suggestions are only a few of the ideas for exploration that are available in art. The art teacher will have many more ideas. Middle grades learners are at an age when they can begin to understand art and its importance in their lives.

Careers in Art

Art offers many varied careers for those interested or talented. Interior decorators are in demand throughout our society. These people work with homeowners and with suppliers of home furnishings, curtains, carpets, paint, and wallpaper. They also are employed by architects as consultants.

Architects design homes and industrial buildings. There are architectural designers who bring their knowledge to a building to make an artistic statement. There are also architectural engineers who blend art and structural design, beauty and utility together. An architect is first an artist.

In advertising there is the union of artistic taste and good business. Advertising ranges from eye-catching billboards, to television commercials, and to magazine and newspaper ads. Designers of ads must always appeal to the kinds of people who are likely to buy a particular product.

A cartoon artist, whether a political cartoonist or one for the comic pages, is an artist. Cartoons try to capture the attention of a large number of people and communicate a message. The message communicated in language is not nearly as effective as it is in harmony with an artistically drawn cartoon. *Peanuts* and *The Family Circus* are known and quoted by hundreds of people every week.

The most important use of art in the lives of almost all of us is an avocation not a vocation. Dwight Eisenhower and Winston Churchill, both very busy and accomplished persons, spent hours with a paint brush. Most of us have a desire to share with the world life as we see it. Many of us try to do it with words but many more of us try to do it through art. Art as a vocation is an important career but art as a avocation enables us to share a piece of ourselves in a powerful way.

FOREIGN LANGUAGE

Benevento (1985) presented a rather brief and dismal picture of the history of foreign language in American schools. At the turn of the century one-half of high school students studied Latin and about one-fourth were enrolled in French and German. By 1948, only 21% were enrolled in any foreign language course. In 1982, about 20% of the students in high school were enrolled in foreign language courses. We are a monolingual society. The good news is that there is an indication of some slight increase in foreign language enrollment in high school and college. In a UNESCO study of 30,000 ten- and fourteen-year-olds in nine countries, students from the United States ranked eighth, next to last, in comprehending foreign cultures. That's the bad news.

There are many reasons why foreign language proficiency is becoming more and more important to everyone in the United States. The main reason is that we are becoming increasingly interdependent in a global community. More specifically, we must be able to communicate with other countries in their own language for diplomatic and economic reasons. A few years ago a Russian sought political asylum in our embassy in Kabul, Afghanistan, but was unable to find anyone there who spoke Russian to understand his request. The potential for embarrassing misunderstandings in our diplomatic relationships with other countries exists throughout the world.

Another important reason for foreign language study in our society can be found in international business. If the balance of trade were tipped in our favor across the world the problem would not be critical. But to do business with other countries it has become important that we negotiate business agreements by speaking their language. In advertising there are amusing stories of our bungling efforts trying to communicate in different languages. In a Chinese edition of *Reader's Digest* the familiar "Come Alive With Pepsi" came out as "Pepsi brings your ancestors back from the grave."

There has been a significant shift in the teaching of foreign language. Whereas the emphasis was on language analysis, it is now leaning toward language use. This shift is very difficult because textbooks are still published that offer too much grammar and too little in oral/aural communication activities. Some states are moving toward requiring foreign language in their schools. Louisiana requires all able students to enroll in foreign language courses in grades four through eight. Similar requirements have been made in New York State and in Baltimore, Maryland.

Despite these developments there are still many problems: "1) inappropriate content, outdated materials, and ineffective methods; 2) inconsistent standards on measures of language proficiency; 3) weak teacher training programs; 4) limited development and dissemination of research; and 5) poor communication to students and the public in general about the importance of foreign language study" (Benevento, 1985). It is still possible to have an exploratory program in middle grades that will create interest in foreign languages and cultural understanding. The ideas that follow may provide a beginning.

Foreign Language Exploratory Programs (FLEX)

These programs run through all middle level grades and begin in grade five or six. The overall objective of FLEX is to introduce students to foreign languages and their accompanying cultures. FLEX is to help middle grade students make intelligent choices about more study of foreign language in secondary school. Any language can become the subject language; French,

German, Spanish, and Italian or even some of the more exotic languages such as Japanese, Chinese, and Russian.

These classes generally meet 30-50 minutes two or three times each week. The content is primarily cultural and can be coordinated with the social studies curriculum. FLEX students can study family living, customs, food, and schools of the different cultures as well as learn some expressions. A serious problems in FLEX programs is the lack of appropriate materials. Teachers must be willing to create their own materials.

Foreign Language in the Elementary School (FLES)

FLES programs made their appearance in the 1960s in many different forms. They were offered in any elementary grade, often in grade five or six, for no specific period of time, 20 to 40 minutes a day, from two to five times weekly. The general objective of the FLES program was to develop a limited range of speaking and listening skills in a foreign language. Grammar content was kept at a minimum with very few students learning anything except the present tense. The successful FLES programs were communicative programs (Met, 1988).

The content of FLES programs is built around those things students want to talk about with each other. These topics include families, social activities, and schools. During each foreign language study there would be included a theme about the culture that language describes. The main difference between FLEX and FLES programs is that FLEX programs are introductory in nature to help students develop an interest in subsequent further study. FLES programs are intended to introduce students to the fact that they can communicate, in a limited way, through foreign language right now in their own lives. Experiences in FLES activities are both meaningful and purposeful.

Immersion

Exploratory activities built on partial or total immersion in a foreign language have been the most effective as compared to the other programs in developing language proficiency (Gray, 1984). In immersion, academic content instead of language content is taught in a foreign language. This has been quite successfully accomplished in Cincinnati public schools where a program has been developed to teach art, music, and physical education in Arabic, Chinese, Japanese, or Russian starting in kindergarten (Cincinnati Public Schools Alternative Programs brochure, 1987). The objective of immersion programs is for students to become functionally proficient and be able to communicate where the language is spoken. Research in Canada over a 10-year period has shown that English-speaking students in French-immersion classes perform as well in all subject matter areas even though they were conducted totally in French.

Research in the United States indicates students do not lose their English language skills after they have been in immersion classes.

Total immersion programs require highly qualified teachers, both in the content area and the foreign language in which the subject will be presented. There is also the problem of finding appropriate instructional materials. However, some materials for immersion programs exist in Cincinnati, San Diego, San Francisco, and Montgomery County, Maryland.

There is an alternative to total immersion programs. In a partial immersion program the total curriculum would not be taught in a foreign language, only part of it. That part might be routine language that students hear in every class. Directions can be given in a foreign language. For example, "Please shut the door" could be spoken "Ferme la porte, sil vous plait." The students throughout the school could receive many directions the same way and find foreign language meaningful as it touches many routine statements made in a school.

A Simulated Trip to Any Foreign Country

The language required to travel in a foreign country is interesting to learn and useful to those many people who will travel any place in the world. There are a few survival questions and answers that everyone must have as they travel to Tokyo, Paris, or Rome. The language and the culture must be presented in an authentic way. A simulated trip for a middle level student to some foreign land can begin with planning the trip, making the voyage, arriving and surviving happily in a foreign culture for two weeks. The language necessary to get from the airport to the hotel, to order meals, and to visit places of interest while there can be learned and enjoyed.

This activity can be presented as a six- to nine-week exploratory activity in middle grades. There are many kinds of materials available for this kind of a program. It would not require a teacher who was proficient in the language, although having such a teacher would help students acquire better oral language skills. Many teachers have traveled outside the United States and could make such a course authentic. During the next decade foreign language bids to become more important in the curriculum. Exploratory courses will become more sophisticated as students become more proficient in language study. The study of foreign language should not be a separate experience; it needs to be integrated with social studies, art, and music.

Idioms

Idioms vary from language to language. Even though a person can speak a foreign language with a native's accent that person must still be able to use the idioms in another language to appear to be as a native. Learning idioms begins with our own language and can make an interesting exploratory activity for middle level students. The phrase "by and large" translated very well into most foreign languages but doesn't carry the meaning that we give it in the United States. To have a preposition without an object followed by a conjunction that joins a preposition and an adjective that modifies nothing forms a phrase with no understanding for foreigners. The phrase was one of several phrases which had their origin in English sailing language. A sea captain who understood the skills of the helmsman to be quite limited would ask him to hold the sailing vessel generally into the wind by using this phrase "by and large." As the skills of the helmsman increased the sea captain would order, "Hard and by" (which makes as little sense as the first phrase). By this phrase he intended the helmsman to keep the sailing vessel tight into the wind. Idioms often have an interesting background but they are peculiar to each language or culture.

We borrow many idioms from Latin or from the French language for our use as mottos. On several coins we have imprinted *E Pluribus Unum* which is Latin for "One from Many." The motto for the United States Marine Corps is *Semper Fidelis*, Latin for "Always Faithful." On the British royal arms is emblazoned the motto, *Dieu et mon droit,* which is French for "God and my right." Middle level learners can find mottos in foreign languages on many seals of states and organizations. Their idiomatic meanings often give a new appreciation for the use of foreign words and phrases.

Aloha is the Hawaiian word for "love." When this word, or the phrase, *aloha oe,* is used for a greeting or farewell it carries with it an especially warm feeling. *Deja vous* is translated from French to mean "already seen" but when we use this same phrase in our conversation it immediately connotes having had a strange sensation as one experienced something that has happened before. *Savoir-faire* has the literal meaning "to know what to do" in French. However, when a person is said to have *savoir-faire* we have an image of that person being very polished in social behavior. *Nouveau riche* is a pejorative description of a person who has recently become wealthy and is spending his money in conspicuous ways. In French this phrase simply means "new rich," but in our use the meaning is greatly enriched.

Latin has also enriched our language with many interesting idioms. We speak of an *ad hoc* committee which means a committee selected to complete a particular task. It is understood from the *ad hoc* designation that the committee will be dissolved when the task has been completed. Literally translated, *ad hoc* means "toward this." In our schools, even colleges and universities, we once used the phrase *in loco parentis* to mean that these institutions could assume the duties and responsibilities of the parents of their students. For legal reasons this is no longer true but there are instances in our society where someone is *in loco parentis* — "in the place of the parent."

An exploratory course built from idioms in our language would include many foreign idioms. Hirsch and associates (1988) said that knowing the literal meaning of idioms without knowing what they allude to is ignorance. "Such ignorance is your 'Achilles Heel' and an 'albatross around your neck'…Educators who complain about the illiteracy of the young but pay no attention to teaching idioms are just weeping 'crocodile tears'" (p. 58). Idioms are important to understanding a language and can be used to create interest in any foreign language.

Careers in Foreign Language

Because almost all people in the United States are monolingual, those who have a second language are in demand for certain careers. The classified advertisement section of any large newspaper will likely include several careers that require mastery of a foreign language. Speaking or reading a foreign language opens doors to careers all around the world.

The military forces ask on the application about the applicant's knowledge of foreign language. They need personnel who can communicate effectively with local governments. The diplomatic corps of the United States always needs employees who are proficient in foreign languages. The commercial and diplomatic interests of United States citizens are determined by how well we can communicate with high ranking officials in every foreign country. Too often, we don't have enough foreign language speaking people in these positions. International trade needs people who can strike a bargain in the foreign market. To regain our stature in the foreign market we must provide people who can speak a language other than English. As long as we require other countries to speak our language, we are at a disadvantage.

As foreign language becomes more important, teachers of foreign language will be in demand. Teacher education programs will need to attract teachers to meet this critical shortage. Perhaps the greatest gain from knowing other languages comes in the growth that happens in each individual's personal life. This improvement evidences itself in the enjoyment of travel to other cultures, in being able to communicate with people who live in the United States but don't speak English, and in finding yourself more a member of a global society.

HEALTH

Health is much more than the absence of illness. Most of us, even newborn babies, are not at an optimal level of health. What happens to the rapidly growing bodies of early adolescents may well determine the condition of their bodies during their middle age years.

Middle schoolers are concerned about their appearances. They want to look like the "beautiful people" they see on television, in the movies, or in magazines. Youngsters 10 to 17 are the special targets of much Madison Avenue advertising. An assignment in which youngsters view an evening of television and take notes on the ads that are meant to appeal to adolescents' desire to look like the models in television ads can be interesting and revealing. An evening's viewing might include ads for soap, shampoo, deodorant, mouth wash, diet programs (often presented back-to-back with ads for carbonated soft drinks, fast foods, and rich desserts). The ads may provide a starting point for a critical examination of the claims for the beneficial characteristics of the product. Students might 1) list the products included during prime-time programming; 2) list the claims for those products that promise improvement in one's physical appearance; and, 3) research these claims to see if they are based on explicit evidence. Ads depend more on developing attitudes than they do in providing information. which is a significant lesson in and of itself.

Bathing

Why do people bathe? How often should one take a bath? Is a tub bath more cleansing than a shower? Why do people use soap? What is soap made of? What actually happens when soap is rubbed on a washcloth? What is lather? Are there microorganisms on one's body even after bathing? Is it more beneficial to bathe in the morning or at night? What do "bubble bath" and bath oil do to the body? Is it dangerous to use laundry soap in the bath? What does bath powder do to the body? Why do people perspire? What would happen if all of the pores of the body became clogged? What causes body odor? What is deodorant? Antiperspirant? How are they different? What are these products made of? Can they irritate the skin? Questions such as these are very apropos and worth pursuing by young adolescents.

In addition to concern about their skin, early adolescents are also concerned about their hair. Too often adults react to haircuts and/or hair styles they consider to be extreme instead of being concerned about the health of these youngsters' hair. Students might take a critical look at claims made by hair products such as the mending of "split ends," the restoration of "natural" luster, the highlighting of color or the change of color (do blondes *really* have more fun?), and the ultimate replacement of hair loss. Can hair be shampooed too often? What does a conditioner do to hair? Would bath soap be as effective a cleansing agent for the hair as shampoo? What happens to hair when it is bleached? Why does dyed hair need to be "touched-up?" Why do people cut their hair? What literature is there that includes references to special abilities that are attributed to characters who had long hair? What are the characteristics of healthy hair? Does what you eat effect the health of your hair? What does it mean to braid hair? To wear it in a queue? To wear it in a ponytail? In corn rows?

Sleep

All animals sleep. Some sleep standing up; some sleep while hanging upside down; still others, such as people, lie down. Different types of animals require varying amounts of sleep. Not all people require the same amount of sleep. How many hours of sleep does an early adolescent need? Does anyone in your family take an afternoon nap? Do you like to take naps? Do you know anyone who has trouble sleeping at night? Some people have found ways that they can become sleepy before bedtime. Some people exercise just before bedtime in order to help themselves sleep, but others find exercise too stimulating. Comfortable, loose-fitting clothing may help some sleepers. Some cannot sleep unless the room is completely dark; others prefer a small night light. Some require complete silence; some like to have soft music; and, still others require "white noise" to mask noises that might keep them awake. Youngsters can conduct surveys to determine sleep-inducing techniques among their friends, neighbors, and families. When in history did people begin to wear night gowns, pajamas, and nightshirts? Have you ever had breakfast in bed? Was it an enjoyable experience? Why is it considered a luxury? Is the same true of lunch served in bed or dinner in bed?

Substance Abuse

Most early adolescents are well aware of a variety of drugs that may be dangerous to the human body. If drug education is a bonafide component of the curriculum, it should be taught by a teacher who has special knowledge and preparation. Consultants and other resources should be selected and utilized with great care. Included among the topics in addition to controlled substances should be products found around the home such as airplane glue, gasoline, cleaning fluid, chlorine bleach, rubbing alcohol, and vanilla extract. These substances are often abused by adolescents who use them to "get high."

You and Food

One way that early adolescents neglect their bodies is through fad diets. Diets that concentrate on a single food — such as bananas — and those that bear the name of a city or an institution of higher learning — are probably inappropriate for youngsters who are growing and developing so rapidly. Diets should be prescribed and supervised by physicians.

There is only one sure way to lose weight. The body must *use* more calories than it *takes in*. This may be accomplished in one of two ways; through an increase in the amount of exercise an individual engages in or by decreasing the number of calories consumed. The latter might include giving up desserts or by eating less food with high carbohydrate content such as bread, potatoes, or other starches.

Eating disorders often begin in early adolescence. Bulimia and anorexia nervosa are extremely dangerous disorders that are basically psychological in nature but have physical ill effects. Youngsters may become obsessed with the slim models they see on television. Teachers must be aware of the early symptoms of eating disorders in order to recommend that youngsters receive professional help before they reach the point from which complete recovery will not be possible. Even those who do recover may experience permanent disorders.

Because most of the victims of anorexia nervosa and bulimia are girls, it might be appropriate for this topic to be approached with small groups of girls rather than on an individual basis. Instruction should include a variety of approaches — including persons who have recovered from such disorders. Health professionals who work with patients who suffer from these problems are excellent resource people.

Teachers might plan with teachers of home living to help youngsters to use some of the tricks employed by models and actors to disguise figure defects.

Mental Health

In addition to caring for our bodies so that we may enjoy life, emotional well-being should also be addressed.

— What does it mean to be mentally (emotionally) healthy?
— What are the symptoms of mental illness?
— What causes mental illness?
— Is mental illness the opposite of mental health?
— Is it possible to catch mental illness from another person?
— Is it likely that children who have relatives with mental problems will also have these problems?
— Can anyone "get well" from a mental illness?
— How is mental illness treated?
— Are all people who have been diagnosed with mental illnesses hospitalized?

Students might interview mental health professionals in order to find answers to these and other questions. How do mental health professions find out who has an illness? What is included in a diagnosis? Must one reach a certain age before one can develop a mental health problem?

Youngsters may know of someone who has had a mental health problem. How did this person behave? What treatment was required? How was the person different following treatment? Actual cases (with names deleted) might be obtained from health workers or revised from reported cases in textbooks. These might be analyzed to answer some of the questions posed here.

Common Health Problems

Many minor problems seem to bother each generation of Americans. Some seem to be no closer to being eliminated now than they were when our grandparents were children. There is, for example, still no cure for the common cold. There's a old saying that with medication a cold can be cured in two weeks; without it, the cold will last fourteen days. Our grandmothers used huge amounts of orange juice and chicken soup to treat family members who suffered with the common cold. Many modern health care professionals recommend the same treatment. They also recommend ways of avoiding catching the malady such as getting plenty of sleep and keeping one's hands away from one's face. Youngsters may seek other ways of protecting themselves from respiratory infections. They might also be amused by some of the "folk medicine" techniques used in treating common diseases.

Many youngsters have problems with their tonsils. Not too long ago a fairly long recovery period was required for those who underwent surgery. Today tonsillectomies usually require no hospital stay at all and a relatively short convalescence. Students may explore the nature of tonsils. Where are they? How many are there? What is their function? What causes them to become enlarged and/or diseased? Why do people sometimes need to have them removed?

Many people develop warts. These are viral growths that come in many shapes and sizes. They may appear on almost any part of the body even under fingernails and toenails. Many different treatments are available including use of carbon dioxide (freezing) or electrocautery (burning away). There are also some over-the-counter solutions that are advertised as effective in dissolving warts. Youngsters may seek to determine the "old wives' tales" about warts and the scientifically proven causes.

Poison Ivy

Many youngsters have had poison ivy at one time or another. People continue to be amused by stories about camping trips and other vacations being ruined by the terrible itching caused by irritation from this plant.

Students may learn to identify poison ivy with its cluster of three notched leaves — two opposite each other with a third one growing out between them at the tip of the stalk. Students may find answers to questions such as the following:

— What is the "poison" associated with the plant?
— Is everyone who comes in contact with poison ivy susceptible to its irritation?
— Are some people more susceptible than are others?
— What does the rash look like?
— Can it spread from one person to another?
— Can it be spread by pets that may come in contact with the plant?
— How is it treated today?
— How was it treated twenty years ago?
— What are some of the treatments associated with folk medicine?
— How might one protect oneself if it is impossible to avoid contact with the plant?

Hiccups

Nearly every human being has experienced this problem. It is caused by a spasm of the diaphragm that results from an irritation of the nerves controlling it. The sound of hiccups is caused by a spasmodic intake of a small count of air that makes a peculiar noise as the glottis shuts. All "cures" are based on the same principle — a decrease in the amount of oxygen taken in from the air and an increase in the amount of carbon dioxide in the blood. Specific treatments include breathing into a paper bag, holding one's breath, or taking nine consecutive swallows of a liquid without pausing to inhale.

Youngsters might interview family members, friends, and/or neighbors as to their favorite cures for hiccups. They might also look into folk medicine treatments. Are there severe cases that require a physician's care? What types of treatment may be required?

Health Hazards

There are many substances and many practices that may be quite hazardous to our health. There are some that are fairly obvious, such as air and water pollution and radon in our homes. But there are many that are not as well-publicized but are just as hazardous. For example, corrosion may build up on aluminum pans. Food cooked in these pans may absorb the metal, which builds up in the body. Over a period of time, brain and nerve cells may be damaged or killed and kidney function may be impaired. Another example is in the buildup of toxins in tap water over night. One way of combating this problem is by allowing tap water to run for a few minutes before filling a container.

What are some other possible hazards?. Students may investigate dangers represented by foam insulation (that may release formaldehyde gas), electric blankets and heating pads, hair dye, cosmetics such as mascara, the toxic parts of foods (apricot and plum pits, apple seeds, morning glory seeds), cut flowers (that may contain high levels of pesticides), and copper cooking utensils that are unlined. There is also danger from taking some kinds of medications along with other kinds (including supplementary vitamins), and the overuse of aspirin, nasal spray, and eyedrops.

What other health hazards might be present in our homes? Are there some that may be caused by products we use almost every day? What are some of the dangers of lead poisoning from paints and from metal pipes and utensils?

What may happen if food is exposed to the air for an extended period of time? Why should tooth brushes be kept covered when not in use? How can they be covered?

Why should we wash our hands after using the toilet and each time we handle food? Why should all eating and cooking utensils be cleaned with detergent and hot water? Are there times when something as seemingly safe as ice water may prove to be a health hazard? Middle school students may interview public health personnel to identify still other hazards.

Health Fallacies

There are many popular beliefs about health remedies and practices that have been widely accepted for many generations. Some of them have been proven to be true; others may not only be untrue, they may be dangerous. An example of a dangerous health fallacy concerns the consumption of milk. The amount of butterfat in whole milk may contribute excessive amounts of fat to the diet. Many people who suffer from stomach ulcers believe that drinking milk will ease the pain of an ulcer. This is untrue.

Youngsters may identify other health fallacies that relate to foods. They may examine products that advertise the terms "low-fat," "low-cholesterol," or "light" (sometimes "lite") on their labels to determine the actual amounts of fat, calories, and sodium in these products.

Still other fallacies may include those that relate to left-handedness (4% to 10% of the population) and the health defects that may be associated with it. Interviews with left-handed students, teachers, family members, and neighbors might result in some interesting findings as to the problems they encounter. Surveys of handedness among students in the middle school would provide opportunities to involve math, science, language arts, and social studies.

Investigation of the use of salt tablets and the high sugar content in soft drinks to combat heat exhaustion and/or heat stroke may provide avenues leading to the discovery of other little known health fallacies. Dangers presented by the excessive use of both heat and air-conditioning may also prove to be an interesting topic.

Phobias

Phobias are abnormal and excessive dreads or fears. Usually these fears are centered around a specific classification of certain phenomena or experiences. People who suffer from phobias usually function quite normally except when they are confronted with that of which they have the dread or fear.

There are scores of specific phobias each with its own medical name. One of the most common is claustrophobia, the fear of being closed in or confined to small spaces. People who suffer from claustrophobia may express concern that elevators may malfunction between floors and they will be held in a small space. Some people who suffer from this phobia will not sit in the middle of a row in an auditorium for fear that they will be trapped in case of an emergency. People with acrophobia fear heights. These individuals fear looking down from tall buildings, getting stuck at the top of a ferris wheel, or experiencing the sudden drop that is typical of roller coaster rides.

Students may want to interview a psychologist or psychiatrist who treats patients who suffer from a variety of phobias. What causes phobias? How are sufferers treated? The root of the medical term for each type of phobia indicates the object of the fear. Students may be curious as to the object of fear in each of the following phobias: agoraphobia (open spaces), androphobia (men), cynophobia (dogs), hemophobia (blood), osmophobia (odors), pyrophobia (fire), and triskaidekaphobia (fear of the number *13*). They may identify these and seek the names of others.

Fitness

Fitness is the ability to cope successfully with one's environment. It permits one to enjoy life. If is not a single attribute but it is in reality a combination of many factors. Basically, fitness relates to the performance of muscles and joints. More than 600 muscles enable the early adolescent to smile, sit, eat, throw a baseball, kick a soccer ball, swing a tennis racket, and play video games. How well a muscle performs depends on strength and endurance — but not necessarily on the mass of the muscle. Strength is the maximum force a muscle can apply. This may be isotonic (the force applied against a fixed object) or isometric (force applied through the full range of movement of a muscle or isokinetic, a combination of the two. Muscular endurance is the ability for a muscle to perform for a period of time.

There are internal muscles that must also be kept fit. The heart, which functions throughout one's life must be kept strong if it is to keep blood circulating through the body. What other internal muscles are there in the human body?

The body requires oxygen, glycogen (fuel for the muscles), and water. The length of time during which a muscle can work is dependent on the efficiency of performance of the heart and the lungs. People who are physically fit have greater lung capacity and stronger hearts than do other people. People differ in their abilities to become fit and to remain in that condition even if all people were placed on the same excellent fitness program. A major difference is related to age. Speed is greatest in people in their early twenties; strength, in the late twenties. Endurance may increase up to middle age.

Males and females differ in fitness for certain sports because of the differences in the distribution of muscles and fat on their bodies. There are also wide differences within sexual groups. As a group females are constitutionally more fit than are men, and they can better endure extremes of heat and cold (Montagu, 1970). Males are usually constitutionally more fit in terms of muscular power and speed. What causes these differences? In what sports are women most likely to do as well as men or perhaps be even superior to men? In which sports are men more likely to be superior?

Fitness can be impaired by many factors. If muscles aren't used, they atrophy, or become smaller and weaker. Weak muscles become sore and stiff after exercise if the individual has not previously been active. The same is true of joints. Anything that reduces lung capacity reserve (such as smoking) or weakens the heart, affects the fitness of the body.

A poor diet also affects fitness. Too much fat as well as an overabundance of sugar can affect fitness. Why is this true? In what way does do these substances affect fitness? People who weigh too much may have excess amounts of fat on their bodies. A strain may be placed on the muscles and joints and the heart may be crowded. This will impair heart function. What are other practices or conditions that may impair fitness?

People who are physically fit also tend to feel positive about themselves. The reverse tends to be true about unfit people. They may have annoying aches and pains. They may complain and be generally irritable and unpleasant to be around.

How much physical exercise do students in your class get on a regular basis? Students may conduct surveys among members of the student body to determine: types of physical activity, frequency and length of time the activities are engaged in, and the percentage of leisure time devoted to physical activities.

Charts and graphs may be used to illustrate the data. A "fitness fair" might be planned to help youngsters to understand the need for fitness (Gosnell, 1991). Various agencies might provide booths that would provide "hands-on" activities at such a fair.

You and the Hospital

Many youngsters are admitted to a hospital during the middle school years. For most, it will be the first time they have ever had a problem serious enough to require hospital admission. Some will have surgery, others only diagnostic tests. Regardless of the reason for hospital admission, it can be an unsettling experience — even for an adult.

The student who must undergo surgery may fear "going under the knife," as adults often refer to the experience. Reassurance can be provided by professional health workers who can describe step-by-step the procedures that will be followed. Youngsters should be helped to understand the reasons that hospitals are strict about routine and about sanitary (aseptic) techniques.

Even if surgery is performed on an outpatient basis, the patient usually reports to the hospital or clinic the day before the surgery in order to undergo tests. What kinds of tests are required typically? Why are these tests needed? Sometimes the surgical patient is given a liquid diet and/or an enema the night before surgery. What does an anesthesiologist (physician or nurse) do during surgery?

Does the hospital in your community have an outpatient surgical unit? Why is it given that name? What types of surgery are usually performed in such a facility?

Why aren't parents and other members of the family permitted in the operating room? How soon after surgery will they be allowed to see the patient? What are the visiting hours in the local hospital? Why do hospitals limit the number of visitors they allow in a patient's room? How long do people with certain types of surgery and certain illnesses usually stay in the hospital?

Hospital workers have developed a kind of shorthand that they use when they communicate with one another. This may be very confusing to patients. Students may determine the meaning of such terms as: R.N., L.P.N., M.D., O.R., lab., X-ray, nuclear medicine, Ob-Gyn., maternity, E.R., M.R.I., I.V., G.I., P.T., and the recovery room.

Careers in Health

In the next decade or so there will be an increasing need for people who want to pursue careers in health. Knowledge about the human body and its care is of utmost importance. Health professionals must also be knowledgeable in science, mathematics, and language. They also need an understanding of and a caring for people in order to provide emotional support for patients and their families.

Many occupations are available to those who are interested in working with health. Dentists, orthodontists, dental hygienists, nurses, physicians, radiologists, lab technicians, x-ray technicians, pharmacists, nurse assistants, physical therapists, dieticians, nurses, and ambulance drivers are needed now and will be needed in the future. Students might interview people with these careers to find out the types of roles and the extent of education preparation required for these positions. The technique known as "shadowing" might be used to examine the daily routine of someone who works in one of these positions. Newspaper want-ads could be used to identify the number and types of positions available.

HOME LIVING

To many lay people the term "home economics" conjures up the image of smiling young homemakers (in aprons and high heels) who cook and sew. Professionals know that home economics, or home living, is much more than cooking and sewing — or as some students have pejoratively referred to it, "sittin' and knittin'." Whether or not the image was earned in earlier decades, today home economics is not just for girls, and it is better characterized by the term "home living." As with other content areas in this section, the authors recognize that many of the topics discussed here may be part of the regular home living curriculum, and some may be very closely related to one or more of the other content areas. The topics discussed in this section are not intended to be the extent of those provided. They are illustrative rather than exhaustive.

Foods

Middle school students like to eat and, consequently, they are interested in food. Early adolescents need breakfast. Unfortunately, many of them are unable to eat anything when they first get out of bed in the morning because of high blood sugar levels that are normal for this age group. Students may investigate the many alternatives available in choices of fruit, breads, protein, and beverages. Many combinations may be planned. These might be used by students to plan menus for their own families. In addition, they might work with the lunchroom staff to plan choices that could be provided in breakfast programs.

Major items in the diets of early adolescents are burgers, french fries, milk shakes, potato chips, and pizza. There are ways of preparing these foods that will render them low in animal fat — while still tasting good. Lunches consisting of unique and interesting sandwiches with fruit and beverages may be introduced in a separate unit. Actually planning, preparing, and consuming these lunches may introduce students to alternatives to the usual burger/fries/shake lunch. They may even try them on their own at home.

Have "Class" at Your Table

One wonders what ever happened to table manners. Teachers and other adults despair of the lack of basic etiquette among early adolescents. Some complain that they are little advanced from the level at which they fed themselves as toddlers. In fact, many parents who have worked with their children on manners would be horrified if they were to watch them eat with their friends. Why should one be concerned with manners? Social contacts such as dates and business contacts in later life may be influenced by knowing how to conduct oneself in a situation involving food.

The unit might begin with the setting of the dining table. Is it necessary to use a table cloth? Should a picnic table be set the same way a formal dinner table would be? How should people be seated (in what order)? Who should be seated first?

How do you know when it's appropriate to begin eating? How can one talk while eating? Is it appropriate to continue eating when someone is talking to you? How should a napkin be used? Where should one's hands and elbows be kept during the meal? When is it appropriate to pick up food with one's hands? If one does not like a certain food, what is the polite way of refusing it? If one wanted a second helping of some food, what is the appropriate way to ask for it? How should one inform the host/hostess that you have enjoyed yourself? What are some things that one might do to repay the invitation?

Are You What You Wear?

There's an old saying that "clothes make the man." The same is probably truer for women — and it certainly applies to early adolescents. Clothing fads have been characteristic of every generation of Americans. Adolescents have wanted to look like Gibson girls, flappers, bobby soxers, and flower children — to name but a few examples. Early adolescents want to look just like everyone else, even the chubby twelve-year-old who looks comical in a miniskirt.

Wearing colors that compliment one's coloring is one way to look your best. One notion is that people can be placed in categories according to seasons. Certain physical traits — such as hair color and predominant skin tone at the wrist — are analyzed to determine which "season" is characteristic of an individual. Certain colors, according to Jackson (1985) are most flattering to persons of a particular "season." For example, a person who is a "spring" is said to look best in colors that have a yellowish tint — such as aqua, tomato red, kelly green, khaki, and peach. People are advised to select clothing in colors appropriate to the "season" and/or to accessorize using these colors. Youngsters may identify those colors that are most complimentary of their coloring, find swatches of material in these colors, and prepare a "color card" to carry when shopping for clothes. It might be fun to identify other students who are of the same "season." Some of the most popular students in the school may share the same "season" with those who are less popular.

Along with the "right" colors come those clothes and fabrics that highlight figure assets and disguise the liabilities. Certain lines and drapes of clothes may help a plump child look more slender and the slender child look more curvaceous. This can be accomplished with "good" colors, appropriate fabrics, and the "designer" look. Differences may be so subtle that no one may notice.

Fabrics, their origin, and their "best" use may be of interest to early adolescents. Denim is a very popular fabric. What is denim? What is the origin of the term "blue jean?" Are all true jeans blue in color? What is polyester? Rayon? Cotton continues to be a popular fabric. In fact, the economy of the South once depended on "king cotton." What caused the decline in the popularity of cotton? Is it returning to popularity? What are the advantages of wearing clothes made of cotton? The disadvantages? What are the advantages of clothing made of wool? The disadvantages?

Caring for one's clothing is also important. It must be cleaned and, in most instances, kept free of wrinkles. What types of clothing should probably not be placed on hangers? The proverbial caution of mothers to wear clean underwear is a good one. This is not to impress hospital emergency room personnel in case of an accident, but it is a good health practice. Bacteria can grow on underwear and give them a bad odor. Middle school is a very appropriate time to help students learn about the care of clothing. At what water temperature should delicate fabrics be washed? Dark, sturdy fabrics? If clothing is washed by hand, how and where is the best place to hang the garment to dry? Ironing clothing is really a very simple process if it is done correctly. Techniques for ironing collars, sleeves, pockets, and hems might be part of this unit. How should woolens be pressed? What are the advantages of using a steam iron? Disadvantages?

Looking As If You Care About Yourself

Appropriate clothes in complimentary colors should be worn on a well-groomed body. What does it mean to be groomed properly? Some students may be familiar with pet grooming. They know that it means bathing the animal, cutting its hair, and clipping its nails. This (and more) is true for people. Hair should be clean and neat, nails should be clean and trimmed, and one's skin should be clean and soft.

Bathing has been a controversial topic for centuries. Our great-grandparents though that too many baths sapped one's strength and that bathing once a week (perhaps less often when the weather was cold) was sufficient. Hence, the proverbial Saturday night bath was considered appropriate. Why was the bath taken on Saturday? Why only once a week? During our great-great-grandparents' days there was little (if any) indoor plumbing and no water heaters. How did people heat water? If there was no indoor plumbing and there were no bathtubs or showers, in what did people bathe? How did people dispose of the used bath water? How often should people bathe today? Is it better to take a tub bath or a shower? What's the best type of soap to use? Should one use a washcloth, a brush, or a sponge?

Clean hair is also important. How often should hair be washed? Is it safe to use bath soap to shampoo one's hair? Does it damage one's hair to shampoo daily? What does a creme rinse do to hair? What is a conditioner? Does blowing hair dry damage it? How does a permanent wave work? How does hair dye work?

Over the centuries the ideal condition of one's nails has changed. In Cleopatra's time Egyptian women spent a great deal of time caring for their nails. Length of fingernails may be largely dependent on the types of activities in which one engages during the day. People who use a computer keyboard may want to keep their nails relatively short. Others may prefer to have their nails fairly long — probably not stiletto length, however. What about nail polish? What does nail polish do to fingernails? What's the best day to cut your toenails? Why do some people polish their toenails? How did this practice begin? Are there dangers to be considered by people who wear artificial nails? What are the dangers?

The largest organ in the human body is the skin. It is with us at birth and when we die. What is the function of the skin? What causes skin pigment? What causes freckles? What can one do to get rid of freckles? What causes skin to sunburn? To tan? Why should people who go out in the sun wear a protective sunscreen? What causes blackheads? If it safe to squeeze them? What is acne? What causes it? What is the best way to treat acne? What is the purpose of using baby oil or vaseline jelly on your skin? What effect does body lotion have on your skin?

Family Relationships

When children reach early adolescence they often have problems adjusting to changes in their bodies. Other problems occur in their relationships with members of their families. Parents (or other adults) may not want to relinquish the relationship that they had with the *child* for the relationship they will have with the emerging *adolescent*. It may be difficult, therefore, for parents to permit their youngsters to take even limited responsibility for decisions that the young adolescent may make. With decision making there should be the accompanying responsibility for consequences. Often conflict between parents and youngsters results not only from parents' refusal to allow them to make decisions but from youngsters' inability to try to understand the viewpoints of the adults and siblings with whom they live.

A. Responsibilities in the Home

Youngsters may be encouraged to identify real and potential areas of conflict within their homes, to analyze the causes, and to seek solutions. They may start by looking at the family as a unit. They might list the responsibilities that must be met in order for the household to operate smoothly. For example, the meals must be prepared; the home cleaned; trash taken out; the lawn mowed or raked; and someone must pay the household bills. Youngsters might list these tasks on a horizontal axis of a chart. The vertical axis might be used to list the members of the household. Then, a check mark or an "X" might be placed in a box to indicate person responsible for performing the task. This may help students to understand the proportion of household duties performed by each of the members of the household. There may be some responsibilities that are shared such as clearing the table and "doing" the dishes. They may also identify some responsibilities that they might share with others or do themselves to help adults realize that they are growing up.

Middle school youngsters may not be aware of the causes of conflict within their homes. They may reflect on those areas in which conflict exists and isolate possible causes of the conflict. They might then list at least three ways in which the conflict might be resolved. An example might relate to bed time. Conflict may arise between the mother and the youngster. He might propose the following solutions: (1) negotiate a 15-minute delay in the time of retiring by agreeing to get up 15 minutes earlier the next morning; (2) suggest that he/she prepare for bed a half hour early in return for reading in bed for an additional 30 minutes prior to "lights out," and/or, (3) assuming an additional household responsibility in return for an extra 15-30 minutes delay in bedtime.

In exploring relationships with parents/guardians, youngsters may analyze the legal and moral authority of family members. How is the authority different from that held by earlier generations? Has the situation improved or worsened? What are the greatest problems today's parents/guardians have with youngsters? What are the probable causes of these problems? Middle school students may wish to interview family members as well as fellow students and/or grandparents. What are the behaviors exhibited by parents/guardians that youngsters wish they could change? How would they want these adults to behave differently? What characteristics of parent(s)/guardians do youngsters admire most?

Many early adolescents find that their relationships with siblings also change during the middle school years. This may be particularly true when bedrooms must be shared. Sometimes it helps to have youngsters identify those characteristics they admire most in their brothers or sisters. What interests are shared with siblings? How can these positive qualities of siblings and their shared interests serve to ease problems? They may identify ways of establishing rules for the sharing of their rooms. This might include decorations, private space, etc.

They may explore ways in which problems at home may affect their schoolwork. They may identify ways in which there may be conflict between the responsibilities imposed by the school and those required by the home. In what ways can this conflict be resolved? Students may help other members of the family to recognize the need for time, space, and resources for homework.

B. Child Care

Next to receiving an allowance and/or earning money through completing chores, baby sitting may be the most popular means of earning money. Baby-sitting became popular at the time of World War II (it was sometimes joked about as "sitting in other people's living rooms with other people's children"). Originally a female occupation, boys as well as girls can now be found caring for children.

There are many guidelines that should help youngsters establish their own baby-sitting businesses. For example, youngsters must decide if baby-sitting is an enterprise they really want to pursue. What previous experience have they had that involved caring for young children? What are the responsibilities involved in baby-sitting? What pitfalls are identified by experienced baby-sitters? How can youngsters advertise that their services are available? Some grocery stores, dry cleaners, churches, restaurants, and gas stations permit people to post business cards on a bulletin board at the establishment. Some baby-sitters use the computer to design and print their own cards. Creative students can create eye-catching cards.

How much should be charged? Older baby-sitters usually demand higher rates than can younger sitters. Early adolescents can appear quite responsible if they make appropriate inquiries and make notes of phone numbers and specific conditions or requests. What questions should be asked? Questions regarding household routine include: What is the child(ren)'s bedtime? What type of clothing should the child wear to bed and where is this clothing located? Does the child watch television? Would a bedtime story be appropriate? What appliances may the sitter use? Will food and beverages be available? Will the adults leave an emergency telephone number?

At the time of the sitting, the sitter *must* arrive on time — a few minutes early tends to indicate responsibility. Arriving with a book and notebook for doing homework also may indicate a level of responsibility. The rules set by parents/guardians must be followed. When the adults return, the home should look the same (or better) than it did when the sitter took over the child care responsibility. Nothing serves more effectively to build the confidence of one person in another than the perception that the other person is responsible and trustworthy.

Having Fun With One's Friends

Early adolescents are, like all human beings, social creatures. Their peers are very special to them. Parties are acceptable social affairs. What are the special occasions for which parties are usually planned? Who should be invited? What refreshments should be planned? What activities are appropriate? Planning a party might be either a small-group or a total-class activity. Invitations might be designed as a language arts activity; their preparation, an art activity. Proportions of refreshments might be determined in mathematics class. Actual preparation of food and beverages might be done in the home living lab. A party might be given for the faculty and staff as a sort of appreciation celebration. Another target group might be eighth graders at the end of the school year, as a "welcome" festivity for incoming sixth graders, or as a special treat for parents/guardians.

Careers Related to Home Living

There are many careers connected with home living. For purposes of discussion these have been placed in broad categories: textiles, food science, personal service, and health professional. Each is appropriate for both males and females. For example, within the area of textiles and clothing one might choose to be a tailor, fashion designer, dry cleaner, alterations specialist, fashion model, shoe repair person, fashion consultant, or marketing specialist. Students might suggest others that fit this category.

Within the area of food science students might explore the occupations of dietician, nutritionist, chef, waiter/waitress, caterer, butcher, baker, host/hostess, farmer, dairy worker, grocer, and food inspector. Students may suggest other examples. Many jobs might be placed within the category of personal/family service. These might include child care specialists, nannies, interior decorators, cosmetologists, landscape architects, family counselors, baby/house/pet sitters, and adoption agents.

Within the health profession there are many careers that were included in the earlier discussion about health. Some additional occupations include obstetricians, pediatricians, podiatrists, ophthalmologists, dentists, periodontists, orthodontists, visiting nurses, ambulance drivers, and emergency care personnel such as rescue workers who are employed through the local fire department.

Some occupations don't fit easily into any of the above categories but are nonetheless connected with the area of home living. These might be hotel/motel housekeepers, furniture salespeople, apartment managers, innkeepers, florists, personal shopping agents, and hobby/craft shop proprietors. Students may suggest other occupations as well as further categories.

What does a person do during the day who is employed in one of these jobs? How much and what type of education are required to be successful in these jobs? What is the potential for earning a comfortable living? These are but a few of the questions that may arise from the category of careers in the area of home living.

TECHNOLOGY EDUCATION

Technology education has recently replaced what, for generations, had been industrial arts. The schools have adopted a more futuristic curriculum in several areas, particularly this one. In an effort to address the problem of technological literacy the public has become aware of its limited understanding about how and when technology should be applied.

Every student today needs to be introduced to living within a technological world. Technology education cuts across several areas of study that include communication, transportation, construction, and manufacturing. Students will also become aware of the many ways technology impacts our entire society. It is a very comprehensive program that goes far beyond the woodworking and metal working that traditionally were included in industrial arts.

Technology education deals with the use of computers in industry and design. How are graphics created? How are new products designed? The computer can develop working drawings of products. Technology education goes on to present how materials are processed and manufactured into usable objects. Included in this educational program are the sources of power and energy with instruction in how to conserve these sources. Students will learn the principles of electricity and electronics.

Probably most important to middle level students is the study of future directions of technology. This study will include careers that are emerging in industry. Exploratory activities follow that are designed to help students look ahead to their futures and consider many careers. All persons today need to become technologically literate.

Computer Applications in Technology

Students in this exploratory program will visit various stores and industries in the community to determine the uses of computers. For example, they can visit a grocery store with a computerized check-out system and one without such a system. They will compare the two systems of checking out customers. How much time is saved for the customer in one system as compared to the other? How much time does it take to program the computer for the entire stock of the store? Are fewer or more employees required for one system as compared to the other? Students could conduct a survey of customers to compare customer satisfaction in each grocery store. There was a time when customers didn't trust cash registers that showed how much change they would receive in a transaction. They were accustomed to having change counted for them. Are they comfortable with automated check-out systems? How many of them check the cash register receipts in either store? What future transactions do they foresee being made possible by the computer? It is conceivable that we will soon have immediate transfers of funds from the bank to the grocery store to make purchases.

Architects now use computers to put their drawings on screens, view them from different elevations, make changes rapidly, and make alternative plans. What does this do to the architect's creativity? How is this innovation changing architecture? Perhaps there is an architect in the community who would be a valuable resource person.

Computers are used in managing traffic lights in many cities. Students could explore where a computerized system of traffic control is feasible and where it is not. The local traffic manager in the community would be able to help in this exploratory activity.

Many elements in modern automobiles are now computerized. Students could explore the different computer applications in automobiles from metering fuel, to warning systems, to trip data, and to the radio systems. Are these systems more dependable and more informative or just more expensive when they have to be replaced? What ideas do they have about further use of the computer in automobiles?

Finally, if there is a military installation near the community, students could explore the many ways computers are used by military personnel. Guidance systems for missiles, directing artillery, and aiming guns on helicopters are all directly linked to computers and their adaptation. The effectiveness of these systems was demonstrated in Desert Storm. What new applications for the computer do students see in the future? Is Star Wars a logical extension of the computer in modern warfare?

These exploratory activities make students aware of the expanding use of the computer and opens up many future uses of the computer.

Communications Technology

Most businesses, hotels, and even individual homes have FAX machines which have added a dimension to communications. Hard copies of nearly anything can be sent to nearly any place in the same time it takes for a telephone call. Students can explore the uses and implications of FAX machines for industry and personal use.

Satellite communications have made telephone calls a simple and practical way to carry on conversations any place in the world or in space. The speed and coverage of printing news in a newspaper has been revitalized. What do students foresee as they look into the future?

Telephone companies have added much to the services available to customers. Many homes have "call waiting" that parents probably requested because of their middle-level-age children. Telephones offer "Redialing" to make it easier to redial a busy number. "Call Forwarding" allows people to receive calls at another telephone when they are away from their own. There is the option of knowing who has dialed a number before the subscriber ever answers the telephone. Answering machines record all calls a person received while no one is there. Videophones which have been developed allow people on the telephone to see the person calling. Students can explore the implications of these services and speculate on new services they might expect in the future.

Electronic mail makes it possible for people with computers to communicate very rapidly with others and leave messages for them when they are not in their offices. Middle level students can log on to many local, state, and national level bulletin boards to receive information or to interact with others who have common concerns. Investigating electronic mail makes an outstanding exploratory activity. These activities give students the opportunity to engage in communication via newer technology, envision what is still possible, and develop technological literacy.

Energy and Power Technology

Our society behaves as if fossil fuel has no end. Students can expand their understanding of energy and power sources with an introduction to some of the research that goes on at Hughes Research Laboratories in Malibu, California. Robert Forward does research on interstellar travel and energy needed to plan such a trip. The distance to the nearest star is 270,000 times the distance from the earth to the sun. We speak of speeds to conduct a trip to the nearest star system, Alpha Centauri, in terms of the speed of light, 186,000 miles per second. At the speed of light we could pass the moon in one second, the sun in eight minutes, Neptune in four hours, and Alpha Centauri in four years.

The energy supplied by a nuclear electric rocket could reach speeds requiring 10,000 years to reach Alpha Centauri. A series of nuclear bombs could be used to reach speeds that would need only 140 years to reach this nearest star system. But these energy systems, besides requiring too long in terms of human life expectancy, must carry so much fuel that they are severely limited for space travel. This has forced the consideration of beamed power propulsion.

One form of beamed power propulsion uses microwave energy that can be transmitted at extremely high efficiency. It is limited by the fact that the high acceleration speed is higher than a human can stand. Another external beamed power source uses light from a powerful laser bounced off a large reflective laser sail. Researchers predict that this power source would allow an interstellar trip to Alpha Centauri and return to earth in 51 years. Other researchers at the Massachusetts Institute of Technology are working on a plan for interstellar travel. Both of these institutions are looking at alternative sources. A look at this current research would open the doors for creative thought about sources of energy and power.

Many things are powered by solar energy such as calculators, lights, and small engines. Garbage can even generate power. How expensive are alternative sources of power? What are the problems in using hydrogen as a fuel?

Students can explore simple machines, such as a lever, which increase power to levels needed to do work. The weights in a grandfather clock work with a single elevation of the weights for supplying eight days of energy. There are many applications of hydrodynamics students can explore. Exploration with sources of energy and power presents many different directions middle grade students can take. These students certainly will face the problem of alternative sources of energy when they are voting adults.

Applied Electricity and Electronics

In this exploratory area students can apply AC and DC theories to working models. They will also work with solid state logic, schematic diagrams, transistors, diodes, and integrated circuits.

In laboratories students can explore with measurements of current, voltage, resistance, and power. They can use actual components to work with both AC and DC power to demonstrate how these different circuits work. Relays, solenoids, limit switches, and stepper motors can be introduced in circuit construction. Troubleshooting faults found in circuits, diagnosing problems, and making necessary repairs are all a part of exploration in this area.

Videotape Technology

Young adolescents often spend more time watching television than they spend in school. The impact of television on our society and on our personal lives is considerable. Companies spend millions to advertise their products on television trying to convince their viewing audience that their products are worthy of consideration. What population groups do they target? How do they go about getting their messages to their viewers? Is product information or attitude-building the predominate focus of commercials?

Students might develop a three-to five-minute videotape presentation with a message about advertising. Perhaps they could review several TV commercials or public service announcements looking for those elements of production that appeal most to them then design and develop their own classroom video presentations.

Manufacturing Enterprise System

The free enterprise system in our society encourages the use of technology. Students can discuss the strength of a manufacturing enterprise system and explore with the elements of this system. Students can work in teams to come up with an idea for a product they can manufacture. Planning would include personnel needed to manufacture the product, tools needed, and ways of marketing and financing. Such an activity will familiarize students with the economic and management principles of manufacturing.

The enterprise need not succeed financially (it would be great if it did), but the active involvement of students in the project will make them aware of the free enterprise system and enable students to experience the strength of a team approach in solving problems.

Processing Materials

Students can use basic hand and power tools to process different materials in an activity that would come close to the industrial arts program that many of us grew accustomed to before technology education was introduced.

A first activity would probably use wood to create some kind of a product such as a foot stool. Students would use a saw, hammer, screwdriver, wood screws, sand paper, nails, glue, and varnish in constructing the product.

Another activity might involve working with metals in creating some product. Basic tools would include drills, metal screws, nuts and bolts, soldering irons, and metal files.

Finally, students might explore plastics. There are several synthetically produced plastics that can be molded and shaped very easily. Using their own ideas they can explore making molds.

Students will learn to recognize the advantages and disadvantages that wood, metal, and plastic each have in construction and manufacturing. These activities will also help students develop safety habits around tools and equipment, all part of technological education.

Careers in Technology

Careers in technology offer a wide range of salaries from blue-collar workers to highly paid executives. Carpenters, metal workers, and factory workers can have their beginnings in exploratory activities begun during the middle school years. Technology education provides an excellent introduction to employment opportunities upon graduation. Many careers will have their beginning in technology education. There are engineers, architects, computer programmers, and futurists who might catch a glimpse of their careers in this exploratory study. As we look to the future we will have to address problems in our use of energy, find new sources of energy and power, and overhaul our transportation systems. New leaders and many workers will be needed. Our communication and information systems are in the midst of a revolution that will revise the definition of technology and technology education.

All young people need technology education apart from any career possibilities. Technology is continuing to impact the environment and how we live. Many societal problems can be solved only if we become technologically literate.

INFORMATION SCIENCES

If one were to use the term "information sciences" in a gathering of educational professionals, the usual interpretation would be that the term is synonymous with "computer technology." In reality, it means much more. Information science deals with the processing of information and the need to communicate it — needs as old as mankind.

Middle school students may believe that telephones, radios, and recordings have been around for centuries. Actually, the invention of the telephone (1876) and the recording cylinder (1887) by Alexander Graham Bell preceded the invention of the radio signal by Marconi in 1895 (Newspaper Enterprise Association, 1991). The uses to which these tools have been put in the past 25 years might amaze even their inventors. Also, many devices have been developed in this quarter century that amaze those of us who are over forty years of age. Included in this group of new inventions are video discs, fax/facsimile machines, and an emerging innovation known as "virtual reality." This section offers guides which teachers may use in exploring this area.

Computers

Computers may be very large as are those used in many industries or they may be very small. The automatic sequence computer, the Mark I, was invented by Howard Aiken and his colleagues of Harvard University in 1944. At first computers required entire rooms for housing. The computer has become so much a part of modern life that most of us don't realize how often it is being utilized. The touch-tone telephone youngsters use frequently, the sensors used in supermarket check-out counters, and the dial-access systems used in school libraries are directly linked to computer technology.

The two major uses of computers are as word processors and as storage bases for information. The microcomputer is fairly versatile because many types of input/output units may be connected to it. When one looks at a computer the major components may not be readily identified. The central processing unit, or CPU, sometimes referred to as the "brain" of the computer, houses the microprocessor, memory chips, and possibly at least one disk drive. Other components include the keyboard, a printer, and, a mouse.

"Software" is a term used for various types of computer programs and for the disks used in creating the products generated by the use of computers. Programs control the functioning of the computer hardware and direct its operation.

Word processing is typically the major use for personal computers (PCs). Programs are designed for this purpose and they permit the operator to enter data, store data for later retrieval, and make copies with a printer. The operator may edit material and move it from one place to another within a document without having to retype the entire document. Many word-processing programs provide for reformatting the text through changes in line spacing, size of type, and length of pages.

Many middle school students are quite familiar with word processing, but they may not have considered the uses of the word-processing function in relationship to the various content areas. For example, combining the telephone (through a modem) with a computer may provide for electronic mail to be transmitted from one physical location to another without use of an envelope and a stamp. How might this procedure aid communication between different schools, members of a family, or between friends?

Computer networks have been developed that make it possible for people with similar interests to share ideas, problems, or other types of information. Students might identify groups of people with whom they may wish to communicate in this way.

How might a geographer use computer graphics? How might a newspaper reporter transmit information to a central location by telephone without having to dictate the copy to an editor? To what uses might a health professional put the computer? The attorney? The dietician? The fashion designer? These are questions that may intrigue students.

Another function of the computer is for information storage and retrieval. Institutions and agencies that have the need for a variety and a volume of files may use various means of information retrieval. There are many different types of information-storage-and-retrieval systems. Document retrieval systems store entire documents. These may be retrieved by title or by a series of key words that represent categories.

Data-base systems permit retrieval of documents that include discrete fields — such as age and sex — so that information can be retrieved through these categories — such as the identification of all twelve-year-olds who live in the same postal zip code.

Reference retrieval systems store references to documents. Through the use of these systems a list of documents that refer to a particular topic may be created and printed on a list. If an individual were interested in a list of books, films, tapes, and periodicals that were related to middle schools, for example, such a system could provide this index.

Radio

One of the oldest means of telecommunication is the radio. Telecommunications is often defined as "communication at a distance beyond the range of unaided hearing or eyesight" (Macaulay, 1988, p. 250). Light, electricity, and radio waves are the usual means of carrying signals because they permit instant transmission. Radio technology requires a transmitter and a receiver. The radio wave has a specific frequency or wavelength. Frequency is a measurement of the number of waves transmitted per second. Wavelength is the length of a complete wave as measured in meters.

Radio receivers such as the ones found in our homes are really transmitters in reverse. Radio waves strike the antenna. An individual selects the radio station to which he/she wishes to listen by turning on the set and adjusting the dial (tuning) to the desired station.

The following questions will help students explore this area. What kinds of programs are more appropriate for radio transmission than for any other medium? Why? With what other media can radio be combined for an innovative approach to presentation? How many different kinds of radios are there?

Students may produce their own radio programs based on stories they have written. Use of appropriate background music and sound effects may enhance these broadcasts.

Television

Television is so much a part of the lives of early adolescents that it may appear to be thoroughly understood by most middle school students. However, for many students the television set represents a passive means of entertainment, and little thought has been given to the technology itself or to the potential uses of television. Many middle schools now have their own closed-circuit television systems. Full use of these systems has only begun. Some are being used for in-school news programs, for presentation to several classrooms simultaneously by special guests, and for announcements that must be made during the school day.

A television transmission is composed of a sequence of 30 still images per second. The human eye merges these images into a moving picture in a way similar to that of a motion picture. If the television picture is in color, three images of each still picture are produced in red, blue, and green. Images are formed on tubes that convert the light in the image into an electronic signal. Each image is split into 525 horizontal lines. An electric signal whose voltage varies with the brightness of the image on each line is transmitted. The signals from each of the three tubes are combined into a single electronic video signal that comes into individual homes.

A television receiver, or set, receives a video signal from a television station. It operates like a television camera in reverse by forming a series of still pictures on a screen. It builds up a picture in horizontal lines across the screen. Red, blue, and green stripes make up the picture. At an appropriate viewing distance the lines and stripes can't be discerned by the human eye. The audience sees them as a sharp, full color picture (Macaulay, 1988).

Educational television (ETV) has greatly improved since it was first used. Teachers who tuned in to ETV in the 1950s often watched a "talking head," a person sitting at a desk or table talking to a camera. At other times a film was broadcast. Today ETV programs are among the most sophisticated available.

Students can view commercial and educational television programs in order to compare and contrast them on the basis of acting, scenery, lighting, and editing. They may investigate the means of financing such programs.

Artificial Satellites

With the space age came a new kind of technology and a tremendous expansion of the scope of the information sciences. Artificial satellites were launched that would provide information about all parts of the world to people in other parts of the earth.

There are at least four major types of artificial space satellites: communication, weather, astronomy, and spy. Communication satellites orbit the earth and relay telephone and television signals from one part of the world and transmit them to another part. They have generally been launched into orbit above the equator. Their 24-hour earth orbits permit signals to be relayed through the earth's atmosphere to permit "live" coverage of events from as far away as half way around the world. Weather satellites have been used to detect cloud cover and to track storms. Astronomy satellites detect heat sources that cannot be detected on earth. Sensors on spy satellites have been used mainly to detect nuclear explosions both on the earth and in space.

Students may speculate as to additional potential uses for artificial satellites. What world events have been viewed by people who were great distances away from the actual event at the exact moment they were happening? How might the course of American or world history have been changed if we had this technology as early as 1776? In what ways have our lives been changed because we have access to these powerful tools?

Telephone Technology

To many parents it may seem that their early adolescent has suddenly discovered the telephone. It seems to have become the lifeline to best friends — the ones they left no more than 10 minutes earlier. Important decisions must be made: what to wear to school tomorrow, the correct answer to the fifth problem in math, and/or in whom the latest "heartthrob" is interested and/or is talking to.

Most of us are dependent on the telephone at one time or another. We take the service for granted until something goes wrong. Then we are impatient to have things fixed. Few of us ever give a thought to the instrument into which we speak or the process of making a telephone call.

Most middle school students understand that telephones transmit and receive messages via wires in electric circuits. Many will be aware that the modern telephone is based on the device invented by Alexander Graham Bell in 1876. However, most students (and adults) are unaware that the basic components of our telephones are a transmitter (a carbon microphone containing loosely packed carbon grains) and a loudspeaker in the earpiece. When one speaks into the telephone, the diaphragm in the transmitter vibrates, causing the carbon grains to become compressed and released. This causes the current flowing through the microphone to vary. The current, when it is transmitted to a distant telephone receiver, causes the diaphragm in the other instrument to vibrate in response to the fluctuation caused by the magnetic field. The vibration of the diaphragm causes sounds which replicate the speaker's voice.

Middle school students may wish to read about the life and inventions of Alexander Graham Bell. Why was Bell interested in communication? What obstacles did he overcome in his work with the telephone? What telephone services and products bear his name?

The far-reaching effects of telephone technology might be explored in order to identify potential future uses. With the use of coaxial cables and fiber-optic lines that can be buried underground the lines of telephone poles that were once a part of most vistas have all but disappeared. Students might arrange to observe the process of installing cables. Lines and cables may have been used across large bodies of water. What uses of technology are being utilized today to transmit telephone calls over great expanses of land and/or water? How have artificial satellites been used for this purpose? How do phones in airplanes work? How have microwaves been used? How have automatic switching systems been used? How do special telephone services such as call waiting, call forwarding, call screening, call block, repeat dialing, and call return work? What is multi-plexing? How do answering machines work? What are the advantages of using answering machines? Are there ways of retrieving the messages by using another telephone that is a long distance away?

Cellular Phones

It is not unusual today to observe drivers of motor vehicles talking into "car" phones. The correct term for this type of telephone is "cellular." The Columbia Encyclopedia (1989) defines this innovation as " a mobile telephone system that uses small geographical areas known as cells with transmitters and receivers as bases for operation within a given area, such as a city" (p.146). Users can initiate or receive telephone calls almost anywhere the phone is located. Some tele-phones are installed on a somewhat permanent basis. These may receive their power from the battery of the automobile. Others may be transportable in that they may be taken from one location to another — including from one car to another. These phones may also work on batteries. Students might interview users of both types. What are the advantages and disadvantages of each type?

Why do people need cellular phones? How expensive are they? Can someone place a call from a home or office to a cellular phone? Is it possible for someone with a cellular phone to make both regular and long-distance calls?

Facsimile (Fax) Machines

Many students may not be aware that a fax machine transmits copies of printed pages over telephone lines. The machine scans a page, making an electronic representation of the material on the page. It then compresses the data to save time required for transmission and transmits it to another fax machine. The machine receiving the signal decrypts the message and makes a facsimile (ordinarily using a built-in printer) of the original page.

Middle school students might visit a business that uses a fax machine to observe it in use and to interview users regarding the advantages and disadvantages of such equipment. How quickly can the fax be transmitted? Why is the "fax number" different from the regular telephone number? Must someone be present at the receiving site to accept the signal? Can pictures be transmitted?

Youngsters might explore the uses for fax machines. How might fax machines be used for planning medical treatment? What businesses might find greater use for facsimiles than might others? When might a fax copy be considered a superior means of transmitting messages than a "hard" copy of a message transmitted to an electronic bulletin board?

Videophones

For decades scientists and technicians have been working on a device that would permit callers to see one another while they are talking with one another. The videophone will use optical-fiber cables to carry telephone and television signals. Eventually the device is expected to carry television channels, teletext, and radio programs.

Youngsters may wish to interview managerial personnel at a local telephone company with regard to the status of videophones. If no such office is available locally, students might contact a telephone management office in a nearby city to receive similar information via a telephone interview.

Students might speculate as to the advantages of using a device such as a videophone. How might communication be enhanced by viewing the person with whom you are speaking? What kinds of nonverbal communication might also be used? What might be the disadvantages of using such a device? How might the videophone be used to advantage in communicating with the hearing impaired? With persons with other types of communication problems? What other special uses can be identified?

Compact Discs (CDs)

Most early adolescents probably know that a CD is a small plastic disc used for sound storage. The sound is digitally encoded on the disc as a series of minute pits on an otherwise polished surface. It is covered with a transparent coating so that it can be read by a laser beam. The disc is less than 5 inches (12.5 cm) in diameter. However, the track is thinner than a human hair, and it is several miles in length. The center of the disc is the starting point. At the center the disc rotates at a speed of 500 revolutions per minute. At the edge the disc spins at only 200 revolutions per minute. The linear speed of the disc remains constant, however, as it passes over the optical read-out system that decodes the tracks (Macaulay, 1988).

Compact discs are reputed to have higher fidelity to the original production than do tape recordings or long-playing records. Because nothing can touch the encoded portion, CDs have longer life-spans, and they are less subject to distortion than are other types of recordings. CDs can also be used to store computer data in a form known as CD-ROM (Columbia Encyclopedia, 1989).

Students may want to investigate reasons for the difference in cost of CDs and other types of recordings. Other than superior fidelity in CDs, what other advantages do CDs have over standard types of recordings? Tape recordings?

Video Discs

Middle school students may confuse video discs with video tape recordings. They are really quite different. A video disc is similar to the record in a phonograph system, but in addition it is capable of producing both pictures and sound. A video disc cannot be used to record television programs off the air. However, video discs usually produce clearer pictures and truer color than those produced by video cassette recorders (VCRs). Sound quality is also reported to be superior. At present there are two quite different types of videodisc systems. One uses a mechanical stylus that senses varying patterns of electrical capacitance imprinted in grooves on the surface of the disc. The other uses a laser to read a pattern of microscopic pits that are cut in a special pattern on the inside surface of the disc.

How are video discs produced? What kind of special equipment is required in order to play video discs? How expensive is this equipment? How does the cost of a video disc compare with that of a prerecorded video tape? What types of programs might one prefer to have on a video disc rather than on a video tape? How does the cost effectiveness of a video disc player compare with that of the video tape recorder? In the average household which type of equipment is probably most practical for everyday use?

Photocopiers

Most people whose daily lives include time spent in or near an office are familiar with photocopy machines. Instructional materials, memos, and notices to parents are only a few of the items duplicated daily in a school office.

Static electricity enables a photocopier to produce almost instant copies of documents. The basis for the machine is a metal drum that is given a negative charge at the beginning of the copying cycle. Next, the optic system projects an image of the document on the metal drum. When light strikes the metal surface, the electric charge disappears, and only the dark portions of the image remain charged. Next, positively charged particles of toner powder are applied to the drum. The charged portions of the drum attract the dark powder, which is then transferred to a piece of paper. A heater next seals the powder to the paper, and a copy (that feels warm to the touch) emerges from the end of the photocopy machine. Some machines copy in color. They work in the same basic way that black-and-white copiers do except that the machine scans the document with blue, red, and green filters. Then the machine transfers toner to the paper in three colored layers: yellow, magenta, and cyan. When the three colors overlap, a full-colored picture is produced (Macaulay, 1988).

Students may identify forerunners of today's copy machines. These include the hektograph, a gelatin copy system that was contained in a rectangular metal pan (about the size of a cookie sheet). Users produced a master copy that was placed on the gelatin (print side down). Copies were made one at a time by placing plain paper on the gelatin and smoothing the surface so that the contents would adhere to the paper. It was extremely time-consuming to make enough copies for an entire class.

The hektograph was followed by the mimeograph, a system that used a master sheet that was extended over a metal drum. The production of a stencil was accomplished by typing or drawing with a stylus. The area of the stencil that had been touched by the typewriter or stylus was left open. When ink from the drum was placed on the stencil, the result was a duplication of the material on the stencil. This was a particularly dirty process. The ink smeared easily and was difficult to remove from both clothing and skin.

The next major breakthrough was the ditto machine. Its master looked very much like that of the hektograph. Like the duplicating machine, it fit on a metal drum. Copies were produced through use of a fluid being applied to the surface. It was not as dirty a job as using the mimeograph process, and it would be stored fairly easily. It had its disadvantages, however. One of these was that it would be used to make only a limited number of copies before the master became worn and the print became too faint to read.

Students might interview people who have used the various types of copiers. What are the advantages and disadvantages of each type of copier? What can be done with a photocopier that could not be produced by its predecessors?

What other types of information science equipment might be combined with the photocopier to produce improved copies of documents? What innovative devices might be used in the future to improve communication?

Virtual Reality

Although research is only now bringing this computer-generated technology into public awareness, attempts to solve problems using "virtual reality" have been occurring for about fifteen years. This is a technique that uses computers to simulate reality. The participant dons a high-tech helmet or a pair of electronic-shutter glasses that permit him/her to view a simulated world. In addition, a special glove may be placed on the participant's hand or he/she may grasp a mechanical input device in order to manipulate objects within this simulated world. As Rheingold (1991) described the experience,

> . . . Lenses and two miniature display screens in the NASA helmet, linked with a device that tracked my head position, created the illusion that the screen surrounded me on every side. The reality engine updated the way I saw the world when I moved my gaze. I could look behind computer-generated objects, pick them up and examine them, walk around and see things from a different angle (p. 17).

This experience was generated by a simulation program in a powerful computer. The helmet and gloves were connected to the computer by cables. It is expected that there eventually will be less intrusive technology used to generate the virtual reality (VR) experiences. The computers are likely to be more powerful and less expensive. With these advances the programs may become even more realistic and more readily available to greater numbers of people.

Participant have the distinct impression that they are completely immersed in the "virtual" world. They may experience a simulated weightless feeling while "walking on the moon," feel dizzy from "walking a tightrope across the Grand Canyon," or experience the fear of being "snatched and lifted from behind by a huge prehistoric bird." The "virtual environment" may not only involve animals, humans, and varying terrains, but it may include different types of vegetation.

There are many uses to which virtual reality has already been used. Perhaps one of the most obvious for middle school youngsters is for a new and different type of video game. A video arcade in Great Britain opened on an experimental basis in 1991. Because of the great cost of this technology, the rapid growth of it will probably not occur in the near future.

A use to which VR is presently being put is in medical imagery. A physician may use the results of a CATscan to determine the exact location of a tumor or any other type of abnormality. By using VR a surgeon may determine the surgical procedure that presents the least risk for the patient. For example, laser surgery may be hazardous if certain vital organs lie in the path of the laser. The images that result from the CATscan can provide a three-dimensional model of the patient's body that will allow the physician to see the tumor and simulate the most appropriate path for the laser in preparation for the actual surgery.

Radiation therapy consists of the bombardment of a malignancy from different angles. Through the use of CATscan results and simulated radiation techniques, excessive exposure of vulnerable tissue may be avoided.

Another potential use for VR is in architecture. The VR field may be large enough to include an entire simulated building. The participant may "walk" through the proposed building, examining the space, identifying potential traffic patterns, and locating visual barriers. This provided the possibility of "experiencing" the building before the first brick is laid.

On a smaller scale, a model of a house, room by room, may be projected. Walls, electrical outlets, and different types and sizes of space may be projected, arranged, and rearranged to suit the builder and his/her clients.

The potential for military use is extensive. Strategies for attack as well as for defense can be planned using projections of the terrain and enemy deployment without a single shot being fired, a bomb dropped, or a missile launched.

Middle school students might speculate about additional potential uses of VR in sports, robotics, observations of distant and/or inaccessible terrains, and simulated experience with historical events and famous persons.

Careers in the Information Sciences

In 1983 Naisbett predicted that the next "megatrend" in American society would be that of the service occupations. Foremost among these jobs, according to "futurists" would be those related to the information sciences. Youngsters may wish to read portions of Naisbett's book or view taped interviews with him in order to determine reasons for the movement toward these occupations.

Among the many jobs that relate to the information sciences are those that relate to radio and television productions. These include broadcast journalist, newscaster, weather person, cinematographer, camera operator, sound engineer, sound effects producer, actor/actress, film or tape editor, sportscasters, floor manager, scriptwriter, playwright, musicians, vocalist, producer, director, disc jockey, and station manager.

The field of computers also provides a variety of occupations including programmers, computer engineers, secretaries, authors, data entry persons, space engineers, and systems operators for electronic bulletin boards. As is true of any group of jobs that depend on the use of specific kinds of equipment, there will be a need for people to design equipment, market it, and repair it. Many of the careers listed also use telephones and duplication equipment. Also included in the category of occupations that require some acquaintance with information sciences are translator, cartoonist, critic, telephone operator, telephone lines-man, switchboard operator, telemarketer, and astronauts.

There are many occupations in the information sciences that do not exist at this time but will in the early years of the next century. Middle school students will need to be familiar with the information sciences in order to make the transition into new technology. Youngsters may wish to interview persons who work in this field to determine the preparation needed for their jobs, the job descriptions, and the interviewee's projections of how these jobs may change in the future.

PHYSICAL EDUCATION

Some parents and even educators mistakenly believe that physical education is scheduled only for the purpose of allowing young adolescents to "blow off steam." During this period of transition when youngsters must learn to accept, manage, and maintain a different body, the knowledge, skills, and attitudes included in physical education are on at least a par with those of language arts, social studies, mathematics, and science.

Physical education is more than a matter of tossing out a ball and expecting youngsters to organize themselves and play the seasonal game. Certainly no administrator would permit an English teacher to pass our paper and pencils and expect youngsters to learn on their own to write book reviews or literary letters. By the same token, no administrator worth his/her salt would expect even the most accomplished English teacher to work with 50 or more students at one time. Neither then should physical educators be assigned that many students (Compton, 1984).

If the purpose of middle school physical education is not just to provide an opportunity for early adolescents to work off some of the stress encountered in the "hard" subjects, what is the purpose (Batesky, 1991)? It should not be included just so members of the academic team will have common planning time. It is a fundamental area that warrants a full-fledged place in the middle school curriculum.

Jewett and Bain (1985) reported goals for the intermediate grades in a suburban Atlanta school system. These include participation in lifetime sports (with the mastery of one participatory sport); wise use of leisure time; understanding spectator sports and the need for good sportsmanship; developing and improving coordination, dexterity, balance, and other forms of movement; and reaching and maintaining an acceptable level of physical fitness, including cardiovascular efficiency.

Georgia's (1982) middle schools focus on the following units of instruction:

Conditioning and physical fitness
Lifetime sports
Outdoor education
Team sports
Stunts, tumbling, and gymnastics
Rhythm and dance
Aquatics and water safety
Recreational games
Track and field
Combatives

Florida's Department of Education (1987) determined that a goal of middle school physical education is to assist early adolescents to develop physical skills involving a wide range of movement. Included in this bank of skills are locomotion skills, striking objects, physical fitness, throwing and catching.

Some physical education specialists advocate centering the curriculum around physical fitness. Others advocate specialization in a few sports that give students the self-image of athletes so that they will want to participate throughout adulthood.

If students are to be truly physically educated, they must know not only about sports, but they must be aware of their own bodies, how to maintain them, and the reasons that their bodies respond in certain ways.

Physical education is dependent to a great extent on biology, anatomy, physiology, kinesiology, nutrition, social studies, mathematics, health, and psychology. As with many other content areas, there is a great amount of overlap between physical education and other content fields. Creative teachers will find many topics that can be used in interdisciplinary units. This section will deal not only with suggestions for the required program but for additional topics related to physical education.

Conditioning

Television and news publications provide regular data on lack of physical fitness among American children (President's Council on Physical Fitness & Sports, 1985). Many adults have begun to take better care of their bodies. Some are engaging in physical activities that condition the body. In spite of the greater emphasis on fitness children do not seem to be following the examples of adults. In order to help youngsters learn about ways to condition their bodies, they must be helped to learn about the advantages of conditioning such as a feeling of well-being and increased energy for both work and play.

One of the basic concepts to be included in the physical education curriculum is flexibility, the range of motion at a joint. The measurements for evaluating flexibility include floor touch, seated floor touch, seated curl, crossed leg stretch, extend flexibility, trunk extension, and arm and shoulder reach.

Strength is another area to be included in middle school physical education. The Georgia Department of Education (1982) defined strength as ", . . the force exerted in a single muscular contraction" (p. 23). Strength is important for improving athletic performance, increasing endurance, reducing fatigue, and preventing some health problems. The recommended categories of strength evaluation also serve as the content for helping youngsters learn how to improve their own strength. These include flex arm hang, pull-ups, bent leg sit-up, standing broad jump, and vertical jump. Strength can be improved through isometric, isotonic, and isokinetic exercises. Isometric exercises require the exertion of force against an immovable object. Isotonic exercises require movement in order to cause muscular contractions. Isokinetic exercises are combinations of isotonic and isometric exercises, usually involving the use of some type of machine to provide the required resistance.

One of the benefits adults derive from exercise is improved cardiovascular endurance. This involves the ability of the body to sustain a certain type of physical activity for a prolonged period of time. Benefits of the improvement of cardiovascular endurance include improved heart function, strengthened lung function, improved circulation, greater muscle tone, increased hemoglobin, and increased numbers of red blood cells. Cardiovascular endurance is usually measured by 600-yard and 12-minute runs in addition to the step test (24 steps per minute). Ordinarily, aerobic exercises are used for the improvement of cardiovascular endurance.

An alarming number of youngsters in the middle school are obese. One way to determine obesity is through the use of skinfold, using the thumb and index finger to pinch the skin at the back of the arm just above the elbow. A micrometer may also be used. The ideal skinfold measures between one-fourth and one-half inch. Another way of determining obesity is through body measurements. These might include the waist, hips, upper arm, and thigh. Weight itself is an obvious indicator. Recent changes in the ideal body weight ranges have been made in accordance with not only height but with age. The measurement of the percentage of body fat through various means also yields an indication of the degree of obesity. Ideal amounts are 16% body fat for males and 20% for females. Why should there be different percentages for each sex?

The causes of obesity are many and varied. They include an inadequate amount of physical exercise, poor nutrition, psychological problems that cause overeating, and physiological factors such as hypothyroidism and some genetic factors. Youngsters must be helped to understand the dangers of obesity and safe methods of weight loss.

All of the areas of study included in this unit require attention to conditioning as it relates to physical fitness. Stretching requires slow and even movement. The building of strength requires a period of warm-up prior to exercising. The proper clothing (loose, comfortable, unbinding) should be worn. Attention must be given proper breathing during exercises involving the increasing of strength. Safety during cardiovascular endurance exercises requires a period for warm-up, a realistic look at one's goals, monitoring one's pulse rate, and cooling down following exercise. When attempting to control one's weight, a physician should be consulted, and weight loss should be limited to two pounds per week.

Lifetime Sports

Even though they may move into their "golden" years, there is no reason for adults to give up sports. However, many adults have difficulty learning a sport if they have not participated in it over the years. Many sports require the strength, endurance, and coordination of youth. For the most part, these are team sports: soccer, basketball, field hockey, football, baseball, and volleyball. These sports are even physically hazardous to older people and cannot be classified as lifetime sports.

Certain sports are appropriate for almost all age groups. Among these sports are archery, bowling, golf, swimming, and walking. One may participate alone in these sports. Sports that require at least one other person are badminton, fencing, and tennis. Many lifetime sports require special equipment — balls of various types, sizes and weights; racquets or clubs; nets; foils; bows and arrows, etc. Some require special clothing — shoes, masks, etc. At least one requires no clothing — just a swimsuit.

Some middle schools organize lifetime sports into subunits. For example racquet sports are scheduled for a two- or three-week period. Stations are set up for the teaching of badminton, racquetball, ping-pong, and tennis. Students rotate among the stations. The only requirement is that students spend two or three days with each sport. Students rotate through special instructional stations.

Outdoor Education

Outdoor education is another area involving activities that are appropriate throughout one's lifetime. Many adults enjoy hiking and backpacking, camping, cycling, canoeing, and spincasting. Learning the necessary skills under the supervision of an enthusiastic adult establishes an attitude toward the out-of-doors that enhances participation during later years. Some teachers begin this type of unit with adventure activities such as a rope course, group activities that involve initiative problems, games and "nongames."

Chandler, Hamilton, and Ralph (1991) stated that because adventure activities are concerned with development of the "whole" person, there should be many opportunities for success. With properly prepared and enthusiastic personnel, adventure activities can provide a worthwhile component of middle school physical education.

A second component of outdoor education involves hiking and backpacking. It is very likely that anyone who has spent time in a fairly primitive natural setting appreciates more the luxuries of modern life. A week without a "real" bath causes one to long for a hot shower. Some authors claim that an outdoor experience involving hiking and backpacking may build youngsters' self confidence — especially in those who spend most of their lives in urban settings. However, the popularity of hiking and backpacking by untrained people has served in many instances to harm the environment. It is important for those who enjoy these pastimes to have some preparation in order to assure their own personal safety and that of the environment.

Camping may involve hiking and backpacking, but they are not necessarily inclusive. Camping may include a site that involves a tent, a pop-up camper, or some other type of shelter. Provision should be made for the preparation of food — a grill, a campfire site (perhaps a few large rocks), or some other type of cooking arrangement. An overnight trip to a nearby park would provide an opportunity to try out the new skills under professional supervision.

Canoeing is another facet of outdoor education. Safety should be a foremost concern. Included in a unit on canoeing might be boarding and debarking, paddling strokes, achieving trim, handling the canoe under adverse conditions, and the care and transporting of the equipment.

A bicycle is familiar to every youngster. Many have been riding for years; others dream of having a shiny new 10-speed bike next to the Christmas tree or waiting by the door on the morning of the next birthday. Not everyone who rides a bicycle does so safely or responsibly. A unit on cycling might include safety (where to ride, inspection of bicycle parts, use of hand signals), common parts of all bicycles, riding skills, and selecting and maintaining a bicycle. A unit on cycling may culminate in a short trip in which students can demonstrate cycling skills.

A third component involves being able to find one's way. Enjoyment of the out-of-doors depends to a great degree on knowing one's location, one's destination, and the safest and most appropriate route from the location to the destination. "Orienteering" (from the root word, "orientate") means finding one's location, especially when navigating on land (Jellstrom, 1976). This part of the unit on outdoor education might include: determining direction and distance, orientation to the compass, using the compass in traveling, orienteering, making and using maps.

The relationship between the use of maps and compasses in outdoor education and the study of maps in social studies and the compass in science should be apparent. The relationship of locating points using coordinates on a map and the plotting of numerical values through the use of Cartesian coordinates in mathematics may not be as obvious to those who are not specialists in social studies of math. Timing of the teaching of these concepts in the related content areas may serve to help students to understand these connections.

Team Sports

Units related to team sports acquaint students with the basic skills required for these sports and to give them some experience participating in the sport. The rules and procedures for scoring and understanding the intricacies of the expert execution of the sport are also goals. Perhaps some students will find a sport that they enjoy enough to follow amateur and professional teams in future years.

Basketball is a very fast-paced sport that involves coordinated ball handling, agility, and speed. It can be seen on TV many times each week from late autumn through early spring. It dominates the headlines on the front pages of sports sections of newspapers. Professional players are treated like heroes. Only a handful of people will ever participate at a professional level, but some may be involved in "pickup" games as adults. Many more will watch games. Some will listen to games on the radio. Understanding the basic moves, the rules of the game, and the procedures for scoring will make the game more enjoyable for spectators.

Field hockey is reported to be the second most popular participation sport in the world (Georgia Department of Education, 1982), even if it ranks much lower on the list of popular American sports. Field hockey combines strategy similar to that used in ice hockey, the stamina required for running long distances, and teamwork as required in baseball and basketball. There is quite a bit of equipment required to play the game: hockey stick, ball, shin guards, goals, goalkeepers' pads, gloves, and facemasks. Skillful use of the hockey stick requires many hours of practice. Understanding the skills required, the rules, and methods of scoring will serve to add to the enjoyment of field hockey as well as add to the appreciation of the skill required to play it or ice hockey.

Flag football provides youngsters with many of the same experiences of regular football but without the danger of injury that pervades the game. Players pass, receive, run, carry the ball, and kick. Tackling is not permitted and blocking is modified. Players pull a flag from the belt of the ball carrier. As with the other sports discussed in this unit, understanding the basic skills, rules, and means of scoring enhances the enjoyment of spectators.

Soccer is the world's most popular sport, both in participation and viewing. Most adult Americans have heard about riots at European soccer games, and they are aware that people in some countries take soccer much more seriously than our fans do any of our popular sports. Soccer requires running, kicking, trapping, passing, shooting, and clearing. Only the feet and the head can be used. The only exception is the goalkeeper, who is allowed to catch the ball.

Softball is a game that is played in recreation leagues by many adults. It combines the fundamental skills of throwing, catching, fielding, pitching, and baserunning. The fundamentals of the game are similar to those of America's most popular sport — baseball. Softball leagues for women were popular long before the passage of legislation requiring equal opportunity among the sexes.

Speedball combines many of the skills of football, basketball, and soccer such as running, kicking, throwing, passing, and catching. As is true of soccer, the object of the game is to advance the ball down the field in order to score points. Much of the equipment used in soccer is also used in speedball.

Team handball requires running, jumping, throwing, passing, and catching. It combines elements of soccer, hockey, basketball, and water polo. The object of the game is to pass the ball (a playground ball or a volleyball) quickly past opponents and throwing the ball past the defensive players and the goalkeeper to score.

Volleyball has become a very popular sport — one that reached Olympic status in 1964. It is also very popular on America's beaches and at other types of recreation spots. Six fundamental skills are required in volleyball: serving, forearm passing, setting, spiking, blocking, and diving and rolling. It requires teamwork in order to be played well.

Gymnastics and Indoor Activities

The Olympic Games have made Americans aware of the strength and grace of gymnastics. Nadia Comaneci, Mary Lou Retton, and Shannon Miller have captured the imaginations of male as well as female aspirants. Youngsters may participate in individual events or in competition with others. Participation in gymnastics may help youngsters to develop poise, strength, agility, and coordination. There is a definite progression of skills in all gymnastic and tumbling events.

In beginning tumbling students learn the fundamental movements, forward and backward rolls, straddles, dive roll, handstand, handstand forward roll, back extension, cartwheel, round-off, front and back walkovers, and front and back limbers. Dual stunts such as knee to shoulder balance, front and back angels, and double rolls are also included, as are several routines. Teachers who truly understand early adolescents will remember that their bodies are growing rapidly and are not as easily managed as they were in earlier years. Emphasis should be placed on competition with one's own personal best record of accomplishment not with some imaginary standard.

Students who participate in beginning balance beam activities learn many skills including mounts, locomotor skills, turns, stationery or static positions, tumbling moves, and dismounts. It is important here, as in all gymnastic activities, that safety procedures and spotting techniques be learned.

Beginning parallel bars is another part of a gymnastics unit. Assessment of students' strength is essential before these activities are attempted. Mounts, dismounts, travels, supports, and balances are the usual components of a unit on the parallel bars. Study of the uneven parallel bars includes grips and positions, mounts, dismounts, balances, circling moves, connecting moves, and kipping. For safety reasons it is important that warm-up exercises be included prior to work-outs. It is also imperative that spotters be used (two when new moves are being learned). Youngsters should be encouraged to discontinue work when their hands become too hot or too tired.

Middle school students may engage in an introductory unit on the horizontal bar. Included would be basic grasps, swings, circles, and movements. Physical conditioning is extremely important for students participating in this unit. It is essential that instruction be divided into small segments so that students may experience success at individual levels.

Vaulting requires an approach, pre-flight, the vault, after-flight, and landing. Vaults include the squat, straddle, stoop, flank to the left, rear vault to the right, and the handspring. The horse must be checked constantly to make certain that is secure in its supports. Two spotters who are familiar with each vault should be required until the beginner has mastered the vault.

Floor exercises include poses, jumps and leaps, floor movements, turns, locomotor patterns, stunts and flexibility moves, and positions. It is imperative that youngsters completely understand what they are to do before beginning the exercise. Music enhances the execution of floor exercises.

Rhythm and Dance

Most human beings enjoy moving to rhythm. Very small children — even those just learning to walk — will sway to music or the beat of a drum. Preschool children learn to follow rhythm and to imitate animals as they move. As youngsters progress through school they are exposed to television programs and music videos involving dance. When they reach adolescence they may become very sensitive about their lack of physical coordination. Teachers should be aware of this sensitivity as they work with students — remembering to use small instructional increments and healthy doses of positive reinforcement.

In the study of rhythms there are many concepts to be developed including: space, time, and force (a variety of kinds of movement). Skills include: relaxation techniques (breathing and progressive relaxation), locomotor skills (running, leaping, skipping, etc.), nonlocomotor skills (bending, swaying, twisting, etc.), and posture skills (sitting, rising, balancing, and carrying). Basic steps include walking, running, leaping, hopping, jumping, skipping, sliding, and galloping.

Instruction may begin with drumbeats as the basic movements are learned. Use of music may follow. As students gain proficiency in the movements and their combination, props such as hats, canes, and flags might be added to give the feeling of dancing.

Many steps are common to most folk dances. These include bleking, step-hop, step-swing, schottische, grapevine, waltz walk, two-step, polka, waltz box step, and the Highland schottische step. Progression should be from fairly simple dances during the early years through the more difficult ones for eighth graders.

Square dancing is usually considered to be a uniquely American form of folk dancing. It has its origins, however, in the folk dances of European countries from which the early colonists came. More specifically, it relies heavily on the Scottish reels, Irish jigs, mazurkas, quadrilles, waltzes, and polkas. Students might determine from which countries these early forms of dancing may have come.

The possibilities for integration of a unit on folk and ethnic dances with units in social studies should be apparent. These dances are part of the social fabric of most cultures. Learning folk and ethnic dances helps youngsters learn about activities of people around the world — many of whom may be represented by students in the middle school.

Square dancing is a vigorous activity that requires mental concentration. It helps to develop a sense of rhythm, physical coordination, listening skills, cardio-respiratory efficiency, concentration, and agility. Perhaps most important of all is that many adults are able to enjoy square dancing into their retirement years. Skills include those beginning skills (shuffle step, and honor the corner), taught in a large circle, square identification, intermediate skills (such as grand right and left, allemande left, head ladies chain, etc.), and the more advanced skills (back track, weave the ring, and grand square).

Contemporary social dances change rapidly. What's "hot" today may be passé next week or next month. The basic dance steps included in the foxtrot, swing dance (Lindy), waltz, cha-cha, samba, and rumba form the basis for many modern dances. Included in a unit on social dance should be the study of the five periods in the evolution of social dance: the foxtrot period (1900 - World War I); the Charleston period (1920s); the swing era (1930-1960); the Latin dance craze (1930-1960) which began with the tango and was followed by the rumba, samba, cha-cha, calypso, and the bossa nova; and, the rock period (World War II through the present).

Teachers must be sensitive to the fact that early adolescent boys in particular may resist putting their arms around or holding hands with girls. Girls may tower over boys, and they may be sensitive about this difference in heights. Teachers may want to allow partners of the same sex — especially at the early stages of the unit.

Some physical educators consider the disco and other contemporary dances to be fads. It might be interesting to determine some of the dances still in vogue that may have been considered fads when they first became popular. What characteristics identify fads? How long must a certain type of dance remain popular in order for it to be considered a standard dance?

Disco dancing usually falls into one or more of these categories: freestyle (highly improvised movements performed by partners who have no physical contact), joined couple, and line dances. Dances are often a mixture of ballroom — most notably the foxtrot, swing, and a variety of Latin dances. In disco dancing the upper body remains upright while the knees are flexed. Arms are bent at the elbows and are moved in tempo with the music. Feet remain in contact with the floor — toe down. finger snaps and claps are often added to enhance the technique (Fallon, 1980).

Aerobic dancing (usually called simply "aerobics") has become very popular in the past decade although it has been around since the late 1960s (Cooper, 1968). It is popular with both sexes and with a variety of age groups. Many people who have recorded audio and/or video tapes have become celebrities, and many celebrities have produced successful video tapes. Aerobics is not a true dance form. In reality, it involves fitness activities that are dance-like. Aerobics helps to condition the body physiologically by strengthening the heart, lungs, and blood vessels. These activities improve agility and help tone all body muscles. Aerobics can be adjusted to various levels of ability. Activities may be individual or they may involve groups of various sizes. Music used in aerobic classes should be instrumental and have a definite rhythm that is easy for even a beginner to follow.

Recreational Games

A major advantage of learning recreational sports is that one can participate in them throughout one's lifetime. An additional advantage is that children and adults may enjoy these sports together.

A sport that has been popular even in the White House is horseshoes. The horseshoe is "pitched" at a metal stake. This game dates back to colonial times when horses were used for transportation as well as for a variety of commercial enterprises. Pitching horseshoes may have helped pass the long hours for people traveling west on wagon trains and cowboys on long cattle drives. Is the equipment the same today as it was when the sport originated? What famous persons enjoyed playing horseshoes? How is the game scored? What rules apply? Are there points of etiquette that should be observed? Intramural teams of similar ability might participate in tournament play.

Shuffleboard was once considered to be a game that was played only at retirement homes and aboard cruise ships. Today many people in other settings enjoy shuffleboard. It is a sport that lends itself to both singles and doubles competition. A unit might include the history of the sport, care of equipment, basic rules, terminology, basic strategies, and scoring. As with other recreational sports, intramural tournaments involving teams composed of students of similar ability might serve as a suitable culminating activity for the study of shuffle-board.

The Peoples' Republic of China helped to revitalize the popularity of table tennis (ping-pong) during the late 1960s and early 1970s. With the political opening of China the championship teams from that country travelled the world challenging the best teams of many nations. Table tennis has been a popular recreational sport in the United States for many years. It has been played in schools, in recreational clubs, in college dormitories, and in private homes. It is a fairly simple game that requires only two people (although four may play), a table, paddles, a net, and a ball. Students should learn the basic rules, fundamental strokes, strategies, order of play, and scoring techniques. Table tennis lends itself to intramural play and friendly tournaments.

The origin of the term, "deck tennis," may be fairly obvious to some, but students may want to determine the specific origin. It is sometimes called "ring tennis" because the game is played by throwing and catching a ring that is thrown over a net. Play may be either singles or doubles. Strategies of play, scoring, and the rules of the game are the basic instructional components. As with the other recreational activities discussed here, an intramural doubles tournament is suggested.

A visit to a local park or recreation area during the warm months will usually provide a view of at least one frisbee game. At times several players will throw to one another. At other times one may observe a dog catching a frisbee thrown by its owner. Dogs can be trained to leap in the air to catch the disc with their mouths. National tournaments are held to determine the best of the frisbee-catching canines. What is the origin of the game? From what country did it come? Frisbee is a graceful game that requires only the disc and two people (or an owner and his/her dog). It can be learned fairly easily and can provide successful experiences for students after only minimal instruction time.

Croquet, a game that involves hitting a ball through arches to hit a stake, was once considered a genteel game played only by aristocrats. A few decades ago it became popular because it could be played by families on their own lawns. Today croquet is making a bit of a comeback.

Track and Field

Events that fit this unit — dashes, runs, and field events — are probably as old as mankind — at least as old as recorded history. One can imagine children and adults in very early times competing to see who was the swiftest runner. Barriers such as fallen trees and boulders may have been added to make the races more interesting. The throwing of objects for distance and accuracy may have been added later.

The ancient Greeks laid the foundation for modern track and field events with their first Olympic Festival in 776 B.C. This event was held every four years until 394 A.D. The modern Olympic Games began in 1898 for the purpose of restoring the ancient competition between the nations of the world. Although many events have been added in this century, the major events are still those that involve track and field. The games are opened officially by a runner who carries a torch that was ignited in Greece. The runner lights the symbolic flame in the designated stadium of the host country, and the games begin.

Track and field events are many and varied. They appeal to athletes of many sizes and body builds. Distances for dashes are usually measured in meters — 100, 200, and 400. Races are run in a counterclockwise direction on an oval track. Students may be interested in finding the reasons for both the direction of motion and the shape of the track. Students should learn the rules, starting positions, and basic techniques for races.

Hurdles usually are of three sizes: high — 39 inches, intermediate — 36 inches, and low — 30 inches. High hurdle races are usually 120 yards in length with 10 hurdles/10 yards between hurdles; intermediate hurdle races involve 440 yards, 10 hurdles with 38.2 yards between the hurdles; races involving the low hurdles are 180 yards in length and provide 20 yards between hurdles.

Middle school students enjoy relay races. This unit might begin with some simple relays such as those involving running to a distant point and returning to tag the next person in line. There are many variations of this type of race. The type of relay racing encountered in track events should begin with learning the rules, including the standard race distances, number of team members, racing zones, and actions that may cause disqualification. Elements of relays — starting techniques, baton carrying, baton exchange — should follow. Practice to hone the skills should complete the unit.

Distance runs include the 800-yard run, the one-mile run (1500 meters), 5000-10,000 meters, and the marathon (26 miles, 385 yards). Instruction should include foot placement, arm action, and body carriage. The marathon is probably the only one of these races that may not be appropriate as competition for middle school students.

The shot put and the discus are two events that middle schoolers may not find particularly appealing because they are not considered "glamour" events and they are not developmentally appropriate. However, the equipment, rules, elements of the throw, and safety procedures could be topics for instruction.

The high jump, long jump, and triple jump are field events. Each utilizes an approach. The high jump involves a cross bar over which the competitor propels his/her body. Measurement is made perpendicular from the ground to the bottom of the cross bar. The bar is raised after each round. Competitors remain in the event until they have failed to clear the bar at a certain height on three consecutive tries.

The long jump requires an approach, a take-off from a point in front of a board, and a landing in a pit. Measurement is made at a point from the take-off board to the break in the sand. Elements of the jumping technique are: the approach run, the gather phase, take-off, air styles, and the landing.

The triple jump differs from the long jump in that the approach run is followed by a hop from the right leg, a step forward on the left foot, a jump from the left foot, and a landing as in the long jump. It is suggested that red tape be placed on the right foot of the competitor and green tape of the left foot in order to help students learn the correct sequence for the triple jump.

There are field events that are known as multiple events. Men participate in the decathlon (10 events), and women, in the pentathlon (5 events). Both sexes participate in the long jump, shot put, and the high jump. Women also participate in the 800-meter race and the 100-meter hurdles. In addition to the three events mentioned above, men compete in the 100-meter, 400-meter, and 1500-meter races, the 110 meter hurdles event, the discus throw, the javelin throw, and the pole vault. Why there are differences between the sexes as to the number of events? Is the winner of the decathlon/pentathlon considered to be the best athlete in the competition?

Some track and field events may be fairly difficult for early adolescents whose bodies are changing so rapidly. It is essential that students be encouraged to compete with themselves in order to improve their personal best records. Those who become interested in some of these events may want to continue with them in high school.

Combatives

For many years we have heard of the "manly art of self defense." In today's world it is not only men who need to know how to defend themselves. Karate, judo, boxing, akido, and "street" fighting are all means of self defense that have become popular in the last few years. It is highly unlikely that middle school students will acquire great proficiency in any of these defense techniques. They may, however, learn enough to be able to handle themselves well in physically hazardous situations. They need to learn avoidance techniques; distribution of force as manifested by falling, rolling, and absorbing a blow; body positioning (for blocking and striking techniques); striking techniques; throwing techniques; vulnerable areas of the body; releases; and, uses of common items (keys, pencils, purses, books) for protection. Police and martial arts specialists may serve as valuable human resources in this unit. Role-playing may serve as a means of practicing self-defense techniques.

Wrestling is one of the world's oldest sports — possibly dating back to prehistoric times. It has been used as a means of settling disputes as well as an athletic event. It is used in one form or another in almost every country in the world. Sumo wrestling is one of the most recognizable forms because of the size of the contestants and the scant attire they wear during the event. Costume wrestling — such as judo and karate — permit the grasping of the costume in the execution of moves. Two styles of wrestling are included in the Olympic Games

— freestyle and Greco-Roman. The latter does not allow opponents to touch one another below the hips nor to trip one another or to use leg holds. Freestyle wrestling (used in interscholastic and intercollegiate competition) is very much as the name implies. In order to pin an opponent, the athlete must hold both the opponent's shoulders on the mat for two seconds. Three time periods are used unless a pin occurs making subsequent periods unnecessary. A unit on wrestling might include: standing wrestling (stance, tie-up, takedowns, and counters), mat wrestling (referee's position, escapes, reversals, counters to escapes and reversals, breakdowns, rides, pinning combinations, and counters to pinning holds), scoring, rules, and safety measures.

Aquatics and Water Sports

Fortunate is the middle school with access to a swimming pool. Some have their own pools, but most have to rely on arrangements with YMCA/YMCO organizations, Boys or Girls Clubs, hotels, spas, or other recreational facilities that may provide access. Every human being should learn to swim — as early in one's life as possible. A first step involves learning to survive in the water — drownproofing. It is possible for very young children to learn this skill. Drownproofing involves learning proper breath control — inhaling through the mouth; exhaling through the nose. Body buoyancy is a second phase of this unit. Floating on your back and with your face in the water should be learned.

Once drownproofing has been mastered, the basic skills, strokes, and diving should be introduced. Strokes to be learned are that of treading water and sculling, breaststroke, butterfly, sidestroke, crawl, and the backstroke. Dives include surface diving, deck dives, racing dives, and low board dives.

Once the basic skills and strokes have been learned and students are somewhat proficient in diving, life-saving techniques should be introduced. Anyone who swims may encounter someone in trouble in the water. It is important that students know how to approach a drowning victim, how to carry the victim to safety, and the various means of resuscitation. It is equally important that students know other means of rescue using flotation materials and other safe implements found near water.

The final part of a unit on swimming might be water sports, activities intended for practice and fun. These include swimming relays; water games such as tag, follow the leader, and keep away; and water sports such as water polo.

Other Activities

Although physical education is often considered a special exploratory content area, instructional activities may be prescribed at the state or local level. The authors believe that physical education should be a required content area at the middle level. For that reason, we are suggesting some additional activities that might encourage students to extend their knowledge and skills that are related to physical education.

Origins of major sports. What are the major sports in the United States? Which ones originated in this country? Were there some that came from other parts of the world? Are there specific countries that are credited with the origin of the sport? Was the game different when it was first played and is presently played in the originating country? Are there certain regions of our own country from which championship athletes in certain sports seem to come? For example, do many championship skiers come from the upper Midwestern states in which there is a large amount of snowfall during the year? Do most championship swimmers come from California, Florida, or Hawaii, states that have climates that permit year-round swimming?

Little known facts about American sports stars. There are many facts that are not common knowledge about athletes. It is suggested that a student who participates in this exploratory activity select a particular sport and concentrate on athletic champions in that particular sport. For example, a student who selects golf as an area of concentration might discover that Mildred "Babe" Didrikson Zaharias won many golf tournaments, but she excelled in other sports — notably track and field events. She was married to a champion wrestler, who later wrote her biography. Ben Hogan, another champion, won a major tournament while he was seriously ill. How did Jack Nicklaus earn the nickname, "The Golden Bear?" Greg Norman, "The White Shark?" At least once in sports history female twins have competed against one another in championship tournaments. These twins also married the same man (at different times, of course). Students may find books related to trivia, sports biographies, books on major athletes, and the *Guinness Book of World Records* very good sources of information.

Designing new equipment that might be used in sports may present a challenge for middle school students. They may want to concentrate on a specific sport, such as tennis, and speculate as to the ways the balls, racquets, net, and even tennis shoes might be changed to make the game more interesting. Students might be encouraged to sketch the design of new equipment, write a description of ways in which the proposed equipment differs from that presently used, and ways in which the new equipment might improve the game. This activity would require knowledge and skill in art, science, language, information sciences, and physical education.

Design a game. Middle school students often have very interesting ideas for new games. They have participated in many sports and recreational activities; and, they are familiar with the rules, equipment and procedures for playing. They may be interested in using this knowledge to design new games that are variations of sports activities in which they have participated during the middle school years. For example, a game might be devised that uses a racquet to hit a playground ball so that it might drop through a basketball-type hoop. Or a game might be played that would involve a basketball being passed and dribbled on a tennis court using rules similar to those of tennis. There are many possibilities that altering existing games would develop new ones.

Middle school students usually enjoy designing games that are often referred to as "board games." Students might select a content area for which they might design a game. A game involving sports trivia might naturally accompany the activity on little known facts about sports stars. The object of the game should be determined first. Then students might design the board and the other implements needed. Little direct supervision, other than some positive reinforcement, will probably be needed.

Bike rallies. Many youngsters will have heard about sports car rallies. They may be encouraged to investigate the rules and procedures required for such rallies. They will find that the winners of rallies are not necessarily those who drive the fastest. Those who follow the rules, recognize physical clues, and make the most logical choices are those likely to win. Students who participate in this activity might design a bicycle rally, schedule it, and actually hold the rally.

Games for a rainy day. Many early adolescents detest rainy days when they can't spend time in outdoor activities. Earlier generations of Americans didn't always permit rain to confine them to their homes. Youngsters often donned rain apparel and went outside to investigate the effects of the rain. Sometimes they would go for walks to enjoy the feeling one gets when experiencing the cleansing of rain as it washes sidewalks and streets. If it rained on a summer day, youngsters put on their swimsuits, made dams in the gutters of streets, and found other ways of enjoying the inclement weather.

There were times, then and now, when it was necessary for youngsters to find activities to occupy their time during inclement weather. There are some physical activities that can be enjoyed in a fairly confined space such as a room in one's home. Students may investigate activities that lend themselves to this situation. Various soccer ball handling techniques, rope jumping, and other conditioning activities might be used in areas in which there is space. Some board games may help youngsters to pass the time on rainy days.

Leisure. It is difficult philosophically to place the subject of leisure in a section devoted to "other" physical education activities. In truth, leisure is not confined to physical education. For this reason it warrants a special section of its own. With this caveat in mind we present here this brief view of leisure education.

What is leisure? Neulinger (1976) defined it as " . . . an activity performed for its own sake, to do something which gives one pleasure and satisfaction . . ." (p. x). He further elaborated that " . . . any activity carried out freely, without constraint or compulsion, may be considered to be leisure ..." (p. 15). With this definition in mind, one must consider not only the various sports, but also the construction of models, the collection of various objects, playing card and board games, participating in or viewing various performing groups (both musical and dramatic), traveling, composing musical or literary works, photographing a variety of subjects, talking to friends, designing clothing and constructing it, enjoying the various arts and media, and on and on . . . . If one embraces Neulinger's definition, virtually any activity, active or passive, that one might choose to do in one's discretionary time might be considered leisure — even if this activity were related to one's work or might be considered work if it was performed in another situation.

The framers of the Cardinal Principles of Secondary Education (Commission on Reorganization, 1918) included "worthy use of leisure time" among the purposes of education. Leisure education, however, has been relegated to a minor place in the curriculum compared with the emphasis given those content areas related to the other six principles. Any learning or skill might be put to use in leisure as well as in work.

The prediction of many futurists that Americans would experience shortened work weeks and abundant leisure time has not yet come to pass — at least not by the 1990s. Rampant inflation and widespread unemployment have not only forced Americans to seek 40-hour work weeks, many have obtained second jobs. In many homes spouses have sought employment not just to supplement the income of the breadwinner but to help to pay household bills. With both parents employed many more children and adolescent have become "latch-key" children who are left to fend for themselves after school. For many children this means up to five hours of television viewing — largely reruns of situation comedies and/or cartoons (Compton & Skelton, 1982). We may be perpetuating the passive leisure activity of sitting in front of the television screen. The concern of many educators, physicians, and leisure professionals is that students are spending too many hours in passive types of activities (Cross, 1990). Healthy people should be active. Inactive adolescents are likely to grow up to be inactive adults. It falls to the schools to help students develop patterns of active leisure.

A study of the leisure preferences of middle school students yielded information that the most popular activity was television viewing (Compton, 1982). More than 3,862 students in grades six through eight were asked to select activities (other than television viewing) in which they participated on a regular basis.

The most popular of these activities varied very little among the three grades. "Visiting friends" and "listening to music" were two responses that varied by grade level. "Reading" was reported as among the most popular activities of 6th and 7th grade students. Although "reading" was not one of the ten most popular activities selected by eighth graders, it was the llth most often chosen activity. This supports the body of literature related to the leisure choices of early adolescents. Most middle school students have fairly well developed skill in reading and have time to devote to this activity. The other most popular choices were: swimming, baseball, biking, tennis, skateboarding, football, softball, and visiting with friends.

Solitary activities (those that one might pursue alone) most often selected by middle school students were hiking, swimming, listening to music, collecting various items, and reading.

Team activities were also popular among both male and female students. This represented a change from research conducted in earlier decades in which it was concluded that females were more likely than males to prefer solitary or small group activities (Ibrahim, 1991). Female students also selected more physical activities than earlier research had indicated. This may be due to the fact that all three of the middle schools that participated in the study utilized coeducational physical education. These schools represented an urban, a suburban, and a rural school district. One school (suburban) was in the Southeastern section of the country; one (rural), the New England area; and, the third (urban), the Middle West.

Educators and parents seem to believe that youngsters need not be "educated" to use leisure — that somehow students will be able to identify those activities and utilize them well. Unfortunately this doesn't seem to be happening. Middle school teachers should be aware of the leisure choices of middle school students. They may use these interests in examples related to the various content areas. For example, sentences dealing with swimming, baseball, and biking might be used in the language areas instead of those that may be unrelated to youngsters' everyday lives (Gentile, 1980). Leisure activities might also provide a basis for a unit in social studies dealing with groups of people in the past, present, and the future. Creative teachers will capitalize on students' leisure choices in their own content areas, and they will help youngsters to see that the "worthy use of leisure time" remains an important part of one's education.

Careers in Physical Education

Many occupations are related to physical education, recreation, and leisure. The most obvious are, of course, professional athletes, coaches, trainers, equipment managers, referees, umpires, and team managers. Teams also need scouts, timekeepers, score keepers, and promoters. Teachers of various types are needed — physical education, water safety, and aerobics instructors for example. Sports writers and sports broadcasters are needed to provide the public with news (often somewhat detailed) about sports events. Park rangers, camp counselors, and recreation directors are part of another category of occupations. Most events that are performed out of doors require grounds-keepers who care for the courts and playing fields. At the periphery are salespersons who handle sports equipment and apparel, ticket salespeople, and those who manufacture and sell novelties. Occupations in the area of leisure education include all of the above and all occupations that are directly related to people's use of discretionary time.

CHAPTER FIVE

Exploration Through Special Interest Activities

E very middle school is likely to have much the same required exploratory courses. However, schools will not have many special interest activities in common. As a school develops its special interest activities, sometimes called mini-courses, it creates a program unique to that school simply because the interests of the students, the teachers, and the nature of the community unite to form a set of unique enrichment experiences.

In this chapter special interests in the categories of clubs, intramurals, and mini-courses will be discussed. These activities are continually being evaluated formatively. As a consequence of being built around the changing interests of teachers and students many changes in special interest classes occur.

Clubs

There are three kinds of clubs — *subject-related, service-related,* and *interest-related.* Clubs help students' interpersonal and social relationships, increase their self-confidence, improve their self-concepts. As they meet with their teacher/sponsor they all have input about their activities. In a **subject-related club** the students already have an interest in a particular subject. For example, a group of students with a high interest in mathematics could form a math club. Here the exploration is somewhat different from that in the mathematics class. There could also be social studies, language arts, or science clubs, Shakespeare, South America, or entomology clubs. They can be organized to meet identified needs or special interests of students in any academic area.

Service clubs are oriented either toward service to the school or to the community. Student Council is the most common school-based service organization. This group can be very influential in setting school policy. Empowering students also empowers them to take control of their own lives. Another service group could be a host/hostess club that escorts visitors through the school.

Members would need to be well-oriented as to curriculum, programs, and personnel. Other service possibilities include tutorial service for students, stage managers for the auditorium, hall traffic monitors, or audio-visual aides.

Community-oriented service clubs can become involved in a large variety of projects such as helping at local day care centers or homes for the elderly, tutoring at community centers, or helping in recycling projects. Local civic clubs often sponsor youth clubs in the schools and will guide them in their service activities. One such club is the Interact Club sponsored by Rotary Club International. International projects include "adopting" orphan children from other countries, and exchanging letters, yearbooks, and photographs with them. Service clubs bring positive recognition to middle grade students in their community. Young adolescents need to feel needed and wanted by adults in performing activities that are genuine.

Interest clubs differ from an exploratory mini-course in that the club is composed of people who have identified a particular interest as one they want to pursue in greater depth than a mini-course will allow. For example, a mini-course on playing chess would include an introduction to the moves of the different pieces, the relative value of each piece, and the object of the game. It would provide an opportunity to play chess for a little while. A chess club would be for people who had developed an interest in playing chess more seriously. Students in such a club will read books about playing chess, share this knowledge with others, engage in tournaments, and perhaps challenge others in a TV match.

Intramurals

Intramural sports should be open to all middle school students. Wide participation, not advanced levels of performance, is the goal of intramurals. Some students who have difficulty being recognized positively with academic goals may be able to gain acceptance in a good intramural program. "For these students a shaky and tenuous relationship can be transformed through the sense of pride which comes from personal accomplishments in school-related programs" (Honig, 1987).

The wide range of development associated with preadolescence creates a situation in which there are early-developing and late-developing students in every grade. There is no way to eliminate individual differences in the speed and manner of maturation. Tanner (1978) said that the only way to meet these differences in education is to plan great flexibility. An intramural program will allow students at the same developmental level to participate in sports even though they might be at different ages. It is unfair to pit prepubescent students against postpubescent students of the same age. An intramural program affords the flexibility needed to get all students involved in sports without the many dangers — social, emotional and physical —associated with competitive inter-scholastic athletics.

A comprehensive intramural program will probably require the reassignment of coaches from coaching a few students in interscholastic sports to coaching every student in school. Teachers and parents can be used to assist in many ways with the intramural program although they cannot provide the knowledge and experience that qualified coaches possess. Receiving poor instruction from volunteers could doom the intramural program. The intramural program must be in the hands of professional physical education teachers who have been assigned the task of planning and organizing a comprehensive program.

Students are usually divided into balanced groups or teams according to their developmental level and general athletic ability. Coaches then plan a few practice days for instruction in the sport. These teams would play against each other within the school day. Students not playing would be onlookers. Every player would participate in six to eight games.

There are several advantages to playing this type of intramural game. The coaches become involved with the progress of all students, not just the few that make the varsity squad. Students are exposed to more than one coach. Coaches work as a team and have control of the program. All students become involved in every part of an intramural program. Competition is maintained at an appropriate level and fun for everyone, coaches and students, is provided.

Almost all middle grades educators and medical experts agree that intense competition that accompanies varsity-type interscholastic sports should not be permitted in the middle grades. Students at this time are experiencing uneven muscular growth and bone structure. During these years each bone begins as a primary center for ossification. It enlarges and changes shape in the ossified areas. Epiphyses are other centers of a bone where ossification occurs apart from the main center. These epiphyses are joined together by cartilage where ossification is not yet happening. Competition in contact sports can cause serious damage to middle grade students during this time before epiphyses fuse with the bone in the ossification process.

As early as 1952, a joint committee of the American Association of Health, Physical Education, and Recreation, the National Education Association, the Department of Elementary School Principals, the National Council of State Consultants in Elementary Education, and the Society of State Directors of Health, Physical Education, and Recreation published a statement objecting to sports programs that included "intense competition" for students before the ninth grade (Kindred, Wolatkiewicz, Mickelson, Coplein, & Dyson, 1976, p. 142). Subsequently, the Educational Policies Commission of the National Education Association and the American Association of School Administrators issued a joint statement urging schools to outlaw interscholastic athletics for middle grade boys and girls. This statement was supported by 220 physicians who had been consulted concerning interscholastic sports.

In spite of powerful arguments against interscholastic athletics at the middle level, schools still experience strong opposition from the community when the possibility of eliminating that program is raised. Parents enjoy having interscholastic sports in which one school is pitted against another in old rivalries. Educators must first be committed to an intramural program . In communities in which a strong tradition of interscholastic athletics exists time must be given to educating the public and a firm stand must be taken by the school district. The two most powerful arguments for an intramural program are: (1) every student benefits from a well-planned intramural program; and (2) the damage caused to middle grade students engaged in interscholastic sports is supported by incontrovertible evidence.

Special Interest Mini-Courses

Mini-courses differ from other courses because they don't extend as long as other courses, are not concerned with achievement, and students select them on the basis of their interest. The format of a mini-course is appealing in that it features hands-on activities and student involvement. Community resource people can be brought in to share a special interest. Students often become more of a teacher in a mini-course. The topic might be something about which the teacher knows relatively little but has recruited a student who has developed a certain skill or gained certain knowledge. For example, there are students who can disassemble and reassemble a two cycle lawn mower engine. There are several other students who would be interested in such a mini-course but perhaps there is no teacher who has either the knowledge or the skill to provide direction for the activity.

There are a few key principles that will assist in developing a successful series of enrichment mini-courses. One is giving students choices. Making choices empowers students in positive ways, giving them independence to make decisions in their lives and also allowing them to accept the consequences of a poor choice without undue penalty. Mini-courses give them opportunities to identify interests and aptitudes.

Another key principle to use in developing a successful mini-course program involves using the special interests and hobbies of the staff as a basis for organizing the options. Teacher morale improves when they can do things that interest and excite them. Students find the opportunity to share an activity with teachers when mastery is not an issue to be a very satisfying experience.

For instance, students enjoy finding out that their science teacher is interested in American humor and is knowledgeable about Mark Twain, James Thurber, and Will Rogers, or students discover their music teacher is an accomplished pilot with a keen interest in aviation. The series of mini-courses is as varied as the talents and interests of a particular middle school staff. It also varies with the recruiting ability of the school staff in bringing in interests and talents of community resources.

A final principle that is involved in developing a successful mini-course program relates to taking a long view of the program and recognizing what its operation requires. The many steps involved in planning a good series of mini-courses all take time. Every staff member should become involved in and committed to this exploratory program. The interests or avocation of staff members must be determined along with the interests of students. When a tentative schedule of enrichment courses has been developed, students will need to be given an opportunity to make first and second choices. Parents and community must be made aware of and committed to the value of the exploratory program. Many parents may feel that any time taken from the basic academic program is wasted time. They sometimes feel an exploratory program is a frill, particularly a part that focuses on interests of students and their teachers. Educating parents and public about the nature of 10 to 15 year olds will lead to recognizing the ultimate importance and value of such enrichment experiences.

CHAPTER SIX

Planning and Implementing Exploratory Curricula

T he types of exploratory programs described in previous chapters do not occur by accident nor do they come about just because a school is called a "middle school." On the contrary, an effective exploratory program is the result of deliberate and careful planning that involved many groups of people — school and central office administrators, supervisors, parents, community representatives, students, and the entire faculty and staff of the school.

EXPLORING ALTERNATIVES

Probably the first step to take in planning and implementing an effective middle school exploratory program is to determine exactly what is meant by "exploration" in this school or school system. The following definition is offered for consideration: *Exploration is the conscious effort of a school to provide opportunities for students to discover, in a fairly threat-free setting, their strengths, weaknesses, interests, and aspirations.* Exploratory activities should be fairly short in duration, provide opportunities for students to participate actively, hold students accountable for completing activities, but not impose mastery as a criterion.

George and Lawrence (1982) proposed that exploration takes place in six formats: (1) through the unified arts, (2) as mini-courses in the required content areas, (3) through interest-based components in the academic courses, (4) by way of independent study, (5) through provision of special interest sections of the academic content areas, and (6) through special interest activities. This view is not in conflict with that of Alexander (1989) who suggested three categories: (1) those provided through the required content areas, (2) through special exploratory courses, and (3) through special interest activities. These three classifications have formed the basis of the suggested activities in this book.

Several issues must be considered when exploratory programs are planned. Bergmann (1991) suggested three areas that must be of concern to planners.

Which activities should be made available? Should these activities be required of all students or be electives? How should the exploratory program be organized, scheduled, and integrated with other content areas?

The first issue requires that the overall nature of the exploratory program be determined. Should a cycle of exploratory courses be required? If so, in what areas? State curriculum standards and those of the various regional accrediting associations may have a limiting effect on the list of required courses. Some states require that student be involved in health and/or physical education for a large portion of the school year. Other states may require sex education, foreign language, music, or some other areas. We advocate a plan of required courses that includes health education and physical education as two separate content areas because they are so very appropriate for the daily lives of early adolescents.

The provision of special interest or mini-courses may be the most difficult type of exploration to implement. This is especially true in an environment in which accountability and the "back-to-basics" movement are strongly entrenched. It is not that the academic nature of these exploratory programs can't be defended. It is true, however, that the effort required to gain support for the activity program may deplete the impetus needed for the support of special courses and the broadening of the curriculum within the required subjects.

The person who serves as the change agent for creating the exploratory program must be firmly committed to exploration as appropriate for early adolescents. Without this commitment, all else is futile. This person should be aware of the alternatives available and know of schools in which programs have proven effective. Reading, attending conferences, and talking to experts in the field will equip this person for the job. The leader should actually experience these programs firsthand, talk to administrators, teachers, students, and parents about the advantages and disadvantages of their programs.

GAINING SUPPORT

Regardless of how knowledgeable the person who will shepherd the process may be it is imperative that all those responsible for the functioning of the instructional program be convinced that exploratory activities are not only appropriate for early adolescents but essential in their district's schools.

The Superintendent and Central Office

Without the support of the superintendent, it will be difficult to establish an adequate exploratory program. If this person is committed to the middle school concept, support may already exist. It is unwise, however, to assume that the superintendent is either open to change or unwilling to change.

A written plan should be developed and submitted to the superintendent. It should include a rationale based on the nature of the middle school learner and curricular needs. Objectives of the program should be outlined and written in behavioral terms. Also included should be a list of specific areas or courses that will be included in the program. This is particularly important in a school district in which the fine arts, home arts, information sciences, and other "special" content areas may be considered as "frills." Time lines and plans for short and long-range evaluation should be included. How will these exploratory areas be related to the core courses? How will the exploratory program be scheduled?

If not already involved in the program's development, the support of other central office administrators should be sought. Administrators are concerned about justifying any changes. They want academic achievement levels to remain as high or higher as they are at present. How might the exploratory program affect the "academic" portion of the curriculum? How would the schedule need to be altered to include these offerings?

Board of Education

The school board has the ultimate responsibility for decisions affecting the schools under their jurisdiction. An informed board can ward off animosity expressed by citizens who see exploration as a threat to the "basics." The support of the board must be obtained. A plan similar to that presented to the superintendent and other administrators should be prepared for the board. Given the right information, the board will support a program that clearly will improve the overall education of early adolescents.

Gaining the Support of the Faculty

The most important group whose support must be gained is the instructional staff — all the classroom teachers and those in the support areas such as guidance personnel, school-based supervisory personnel, and media specialists. Not enough can be said here about the importance of the instructional media center in an exploratory program. Without the support of this area, exploration will be hard-pressed to succeed.

Decisions about curricula should be made by those most closely related to the students. Teachers must believe that the curriculum is meeting the needs of students. They must have the ownership that is created when they have been involved in the planning process (Glickman, 1990; Liberman, 1982).

The faculty should be presented information about the concept of exploration. Groups of teachers may be organized to study the plan and its impact on the curriculum. Faircloth (1990) found that teachers of the exploratory content areas are likely to be strong advocates of the program if they are actively involved in the planning process and are consulted about the activities provided.

Teachers and other staff members must be presented plans for exploration and be provided sufficient time to examine all facets of the proposal. A full academic year may be needed to plan, consider, refine, and approve a new exploratory program.

Parental Involvement

Exploratory programs can be established without the knowledge and support of parents whose children will participate. A wise administrator, however, will want parents to learn about exploration through accurate information provided by the school rather than through misinformation obtained elsewhere. Before a final decision to initiate an exploratory program has been reached, parents should be involved. Parents naturally want to know about the nature of the exploratory program, how the academic program will be affected, how much time is to be devoted to the program, and how their youngsters will benefit.

Perhaps several presentations may be provided for parents as a group. Parents from a school that has an effective exploratory program might be brought in to share their views. The more parents understand the nature of young adolescents and the goals of exploratory activities the more supportive they will be.

Students Too Have A Part

Last, but certainly not least, the students who are to be the consumers of the program should be involved at several stages. If the program is expected to meet their needs and interests a planned attempt to ascertain those needs and interests should be carried out. There may be some justification for not involving students in planning the academic program, but there is none for ruling them out of involvement when this special middle level curriculum component is being developed.

Just as faculty acceptance of the program is enhanced by their involvement so student acceptance is garnered by their involvement. Though a school cannot usually meet all the students' expressed needs and interests the students who have been party to the discussion readily understand reality.

GETTING STARTED

Before the exploratory program which has received support is actually put into operation, a written statement setting forth all particulars is needed; and it, or portions of it, should be distributed to various constituents. Uncertainty breeds criticism while clarity induces support.

School Visits

One of the best sources of information about exploratory programs is a school that has an effective program. Teachers, administrators, parents, and school board members should visit such a school and spend an entire day experiencing the program. They should review any written materials pertaining to exploration along with the schedule. They should observe exploratory classes in operation and interview teachers of these courses as well as other teachers. Students and parents should be interviewed as to their feelings about the program. What pitfalls should be avoided? Are students pleased with the program? What would they change if they could? In what ways are parents involved in the planning, implementation, and evaluation of the program?

Upon return from the host school, the group should report to the faculty. How does the program at the host school relate to the proposed program here? What cautions and pitfalls did the faculty identify? What did parents and students say about the program? How does the school evaluate their program?

Presentations by Resource Persons

If it is not possible for teams to travel to established programs, perhaps it would be possible for representatives of that established program to visit the target school. These visitors should be asked to present a brief history of the program, how it was planned, problems encountered, the nature of the program, scheduling problems, and types of evaluation used. Following the presentations opportunity for questions and dialogue should be provided.

Attending Conferences

There are many conferences held every year that will prove helpful to schools seeking information about exploratory programs. State, regional, and national middle school conferences are rich sources of ideas. Conference attendance provides an opportunity for participants to hear and to see presentations and to talk with those who have developed programs. Materials brought home should become part of the school's professional library and circulated to faculty.

Naming the Program

What's in a name? Do we label fine arts, practical arts, technology, and personal typing "unified arts?" Do we call them along with physical education "personal development?" Should mini-courses be identified as interest/enrichment activities? Many schools lump everything that is not part of the "academic" block as "exploratory" or "exploratories." A few call the academic teams "core" and the exploratory teams "encore." Schools should select their own titles for these curricular areas. There is no consensus at this time as to the best label.

The Exploratory Team

If exploration is an integral part of the total curriculum, teachers of exploratory areas should feel that their status is equal to that of other teachers in the school. They should comprise a team and have all of the rights and responsibilities of other teams — a team area, a leader, and common planning time. Teachers of exploratory content areas must never be treated like second-class citizens — although they sometimes have been. In some large schools it has been possible for the exploratory teachers to be assigned to academic teams. Where this is not possible, special efforts should be made to insure that communication between core teachers and exploratory teachers exists.

Scheduling Exploratories

How often should exploratory courses be scheduled? What time of the day is best? There is no common standard by which to answer these questions. George and Lawrence (1982) suggested these guidelines for exploratory courses: (1) schedule all exploratory activities during the regular school day; (2) the entire faculty should be involved in exploration at some level; (3) if classes meet every day, four to six weeks should be the limit in the amount of time devoted to each segment; (4) if classes meet two or three times weekly, four to nine weeks should be the range of time; and, (5) students must be held accountable in some way so that they will take these experiences seriously.

George (1983) stated that exploratory programs are doomed to failure when learning activities are offered *only* at the end of the day to students who did not get their first choice by teachers who also did not get their first choice.

Exploration within the required courses presents no special scheduling problems. Exploratory activities that cut across content areas should be scheduled by the academic team. Special activities and clubs can be scheduled for the entire school at the same time and for *at least* two days a week at a time other than last period.

The question of scheduling exploratory courses may be the most critical one. What evidence is there that the so-called "academic" courses are taught most effectively when they are scheduled during the first few hours of school? There is absolutely none! Even if there was sufficient evidence, not all students could participate in special courses at the same time. A possible solution is to consider the special courses together as a block of instructional time. The block of time can be scheduled during different portions of the day. For example, at Griffin Middle School in Smyrna, Georgia, the unified arts, music, and physical education are considered the special exploratory courses. One entire grade level is scheduled for the exploratory block early in the day; a second group, in the middle of the day; the third, toward the end of the day. The schedule is rotated every 12 weeks so that each grade group will be scheduled for exploratory courses during each of the three time slots.

Figure 4 is a representation of the master schedule at Griffin Middle School. Large blocks of instructional time are scheduled for each team. The "team" portion of the schedule provides for instruction in language arts, social studies, math, and science. The exploratory block includes the unified arts (art, technology, personal typing, and home living), music (chorus, instrumental music, and general music), and physical education. A ten minute period at the beginning of the day and a 15 minute period at the end of the day are for advisory activities. The schedule is rotated every 12 weeks. At that time the 6th grade takes over the schedule that the 7th grade had followed; the 7th grade, that of the 8th grade; the 8th grade, the 6th grade schedule. Twelve weeks later the schedule rotates again.

Figure 5 shows how the exploratory courses are scheduled at Griffin Middle School There are three teams at each grade level — A, B, and C. All students in a particular grade are scheduled for the exploratory block at the same time. Each exploratory block contains two sub-blocks of one hour each. Team A follows one schedule; Team B, another; and, Team C, still another. This is true regardless of the grade level of students. The order of the activities within the schedule change every day. For example, students on Team 6A on Monday first participate in unified arts. After one hour, these students are scheduled for music (either chorus, instrumental music, or general music). On Tuesday Team 6A goes first to physical education and then to the unified arts area, where they are in art, technology, personal typing, or home living. On Wednesday the schedule for 6A includes music and physical education. Thursday's schedule for this group includes unified arts and music. On Friday the 6A group participates in physical education and unified arts. Team 7A and Team 8A follow the same rotation schedule as does Team A in the 6th grade. Where are 6B and 6C while 6A is in unified arts? Team 6B is in music; 6C is engaged in physical education. This is a very simple, but a very effective schedule, and *no* computer program was required.

Figure 4

Griffin Middle School Master Schedule
First Quarter

	10 min	4 3/4+ hours		1 2/3 hours	15 min
Team 6A					
Team 6B		Language Arts Math Science Social Studies Lunch		Team Planning	
Team 6C					

		1 2/3 hours	4 3/4+ hours		
Team 7A			Language Arts Math Science Social Studies Lunch		
Team 7B		Team Planning			
Team 7C					

		1 3/4+ hours	1 2/3 hours	3 hours	
Team 8A		Language Arts Math Science Social Studies Lunch	Team Planning	Language Arts Math Science Social Studies Lunch	
Team 8B					
Team 8C					

Figure 5

**Representation of a Rotation Schedule for Exploratory
Offerings Through the "Special" Content Areas***

		12 Weeks		12 Weeks		12 Weeks	
TEAM A	Mon	UA	M	M	PE	PE	UA
	Tues	PE	UA	UA	M	M	PE
	Wed	M	PE	PE	UA	UA	M
	Thur	UA	M	M	PE	PE	UA
	Fri	PE	UA	UA	M	M	PE
TEAM B	Mon	M	PE	PE	UA	UA	M
	Tues	UA	M	M	PE	PE	UA
	Wed	PE	UA	UA	M	M	PE
	Thur	M	PE	PE	UA	UA	M
	Fri	UA	M	M	PE	PE	UA
TEAM C	Mon	PE	UA	UA	M	M	PE
	Tues	M	PE	PE	UA	UA	M
	Wed	UA	M	M	PE	PE	UA
	Thur	PE	UA	UA	M	M	PE
	Fri	M	PE	PE	UA	UA	M

* M = Music (Instrumental, Choral, and General)
UA = Unified Arts (Art, Industrial Arts, Home Living,,
and Personal Typing
PE = Physical Education

Implementing the Activities Program

Once the decision has been made to offer an enrichment/activities program in addition to the required cycle of exploratory courses, the faculty should proceed with deliberation and care to implement it. At some later date the faculty may decide to involve volunteers from the community, but at the outset is probably wise to restrict the leadership of the activities to the faculty and staff. Teachers should be asked which activities they would feel comfortable leading (Alexander & George, 1981; Merenbloom, 1988). Each teacher should provide a brief description of the proposed mini-course. Then the descriptions are compiled into an activities schedule showing what activities are offered each period. Minimum and maximum enrollment figures should be provided for each activity as appropriate. The schedule should be provided for all faculty so that they may review them with students before students are asked to make selections. After a few days students should be asked to indicate first, second, and third choices. Some activities will be popular at all grade levels. It is probably fair to give 8th grade students first choice whenever possible, followed by 7th graders. Finally, 6th graders' choices would be honored as much as possible.

Evaluation Plans

A comprehensive plan should be developed for evaluating the entire program *before* the activities begin. A discussion of the process of evaluation, both formative and summative, is the focus of Chapter Eight.

MAINTAINING THE PROGRAM

Even a well-planned program that has the support of all concerned needs to be nurtured as it moves along. All programs require evaluation, revision, and redirection from time to time. The process is a constant one.

Evaluation of Activities

Every exploratory offering should be evaluated at its conclusion. This is particularly essential for the mini-courses. Objectives should be developed before the activity begins and should form the basis of evaluation. What were students expected to be able to do as the result of participating? What knowledge, attitudes, and/or skills should be evident upon completion?

Students should also be asked about their feelings of success in addition to what they believe they have gained as the result of participation in this activity. This may be in the form of a simple paper and pencil evaluation form or through some sort of structured discussion or interviews. It would be valuable to know what other activities students might like to have offered.

Teachers should also be asked to evaluate the activity. Their written evaluations should relate to the objectives, and the format might be either objective/short answer or narrative in nature. Suggested items might include questions as to whether or not the teacher was able to meet the instructional objectives. If not, why not? What obstacles need to be overcome? Would the teacher want to be in charge of the same activity another time? If so, what changes ought to be made? What additional offerings should be included? Parents might also be involved in the evaluation process. This communicates to parents/guardians that this program is considered to be important.

After the evaluation has been completed changes should be made in the program that reflect the data gathered. What activities appeared to be most successful? Which ones may have been inappropriate? Poorly planned? Of little interest? What additions should be made? What deletions?

Changing the Exploratory Courses

The evaluation carried out at the end of a round of activities or mini-courses comes too late to change the schedule of activities planned for the next round, but it should be used to improve the program in the succeeding months.

Use of the evaluative data about special exploratory offerings such as those discussed in Chapter Four (art, music, etc.) can also lead to changes. What were the most interesting activities? How might the other activities be made more interesting? When students are permitted to elect some of these courses as 8th graders, which ones are elected? Saylor, Alexander, and Lewis (1981) refer to this type of evaluation as students "voting with their feet;" in other words, avoiding (walking away from) some activities.

Staff Turnover

Teachers should be involved in selecting new staff. The team on which there is a vacancy should interview prospects to determine their compatibility with that of the present faculty. For example, a prospective physical education teacher who views the program of the middle school as a training ground for high school interscholastic teams is probably not going to be satisfied with an exploratory program in physical education. This will also be true in a physical education program that includes a heavy emphasis on lifetime sports. Teachers who are not committed to an exploratory program are unlikely to add much to the innovative nature of such a program. On the other hand, a well-qualified teacher who may never have worked with an exploratory program but who likes and understands early adolescents may be willing and able to participate in a well-defined exploratory program.

Involving the Community

Community support is essential to the success of an exploratory program. There are many ways that might be used to keep the public informed. In the Gwinnett County (Georgia) School District each school (elementary, middle, and high) has formed a local school advisory committee (LSAC), whose members are appointed by the parent-teacher organization. This group works with the principal and faculty to determine needs of the school and to help interpret these to the other people in the attendance district. A district-wide advisory committee works with the superintendent on matters that affect the entire district. A similar type of committee structure might be established in individual middle schools to help obtain and maintain community support.

Another way to keep the community informed is through parent volunteers who devote time serving as instructional aides. When parents are directly involved in the program they understand it better, are more appreciative of the school, and are able to discuss the school's work intelligently with others in the community. Parents should be made to feel welcome at any time and should be invited and encouraged to participate as volunteers or just supporters.

Some volunteers will be capable of leading portions of the activities program. Some may not have children in the school. A survey of the community may identify some of these persons who might not ordinarily be reached by letters sent home by children. A retired business executive may be a collector of duck decoys and may be willing to share this interest with middle school students. The homemaker who does tatting might be pleased to share her skill with students. An active file on potential volunteers should be kept in a central location.

CHAPTER SEVEN

Success Stories

T here are many different ideas about what constitutes an exploratory program. Some see an exploratory program as a unified arts program planned to involve all middle level students in a cycle of required courses. Others feel that the exploratory curriculum should be drawn from the interests of students, communities, and families. Waltz (1976) described a program planned by teachers in fine and practical arts working together as a team to develop common themes. In 1989 these teachers developed a theme on the United States Bicentennial Celebration. Still others subscribe to an exploratory curriculum that shows a close relationship to skills developed in the general curriculum. Schneider (1986) postulated "… if attention is placed on providing an integrated curriculum of basic skills through exploration, exploratory programs will not only survive the educational reform movement of the 80s but will become the cornerstone of education within the middle school years and beyond." The meaning of exploration varies widely from one middle level educator to another.

As these citations indicate, there are very few established criteria by which to define exploratory programs or to select exemplary programs. Four very different programs have been selected for inclusion in this chapter as examples. Each is exemplary in its own way; each offers students exciting and worthwhile experiences in school.

DANIEL MORGAN MIDDLE SCHOOL, WINCHESTER, VIRGINIA

A unique characteristic of the exploratory program at Daniel Morgan Middle School is that it is scheduled for everyone right in the middle of a seven-period day. A fifty-minute period offers a break in the tedium of the academic day and gives all students an opportunity to do something they have selected to do. There are, of course, other characteristics that make the program at Daniel Morgan an exemplary one. An Activity Coordinator, charged with making the schedule, works closely with a Faculty Computer Specialist. Every six weeks during the year a specific sequence of steps takes place: teachers indicate in a published list what activity they would like to direct; students indicate their preferences; students are registered; and a roster is published and distributed.

The origin of this program is interesting. All music, intramurals, and clubs had been scheduled outside the regular school day for a dwindling number of students. Students weren't able to arrange transportation after school. It was determined that band needed to be scheduled during the regular school day if there was to be a band. This determination was coupled with a self-study in 1980 that recommended that all school resources — time, space, personnel — should be used to better advantage. The outgrowth of this study was a flexible schedule developed around the lunch period that enabled the scheduling of all activities.

There was great apprehension in the beginning. Many teachers had little hope that this plan would ever work. However, feelings of doubt were short-lived. The program was an immediate success with students and teachers alike. The faculty saw the new exploratory program as an important part of the total curriculum and a significant contribution to a positive school climate. This success could be partially attributed to the fact there was an Activity Coordinator who accepted responsibility to make it work.

Each six weeks students register for two activities from a published list of mini-courses. One of these activities is scheduled for two days, Tuesdays and Thursdays, and the other for three days, Mondays, Wednesdays, and Fridays. There are a few activities, such as band, chorus, Future Homemakers of America, Technology Student Association, and newspaper and yearbook that extend beyond a single six-week period, but most offerings are limited to six weeks. Teachers alternate between a two-day and a three-day activity in successive six-weeks periods.

Computer technology gets much credit for making this program possible. The rapid turn-around time with a new list of activities every six weeks makes the use of the computer necessary. All students, including those in special education, are involved in these exploratory activities. Students indicate a priority of choices from which a master schedule is organized. This master schedule is broken down by home bases to notify students where they will be enrolled for the next six-weeks period. This same master schedule is rewritten for the exploratory teachers to advise them about the students assigned to their activities. It is easy to see that the computer is essential to this program. The Faculty Computer Specialist at Daniel Morgan is central to the smooth running of the program.

Many benefits come from this type of exploratory program. The fourth period enrichment offerings at Daniel Morgan Middle School bring a break in the middle of the day. After this refreshing interlude teachers and students are ready to resume their ongoing tasks. There are other benefits cited for this exploratory program. It provides many opportunities for social interaction between student and teacher and among students in a non-graded environment. Students need such opportunities which are often not available during the school day. Teachers enjoy having an opportunity to direct an activity in an interest area or hobby. Students really enjoy seeing their teachers in a different light and are surprised to see them doing anything other than their subjects. It is also very beneficial for students to be able to make their own choices. The wide variety of activities available to students each six weeks increases their awareness and knowledge of many areas that they would not have pursued on their own. Within the last six years at Daniel Morgan there have been more than 143 exploratory offerings from which students could make their selections.

To illustrate the range of offerings at Daniel Morgan Middle School, during the second six-weeks period one year the following twenty-eight (28) different activities were scheduled:

Carmen Sandiego : With a computer, travel throughout the U.S.A. using historical and geographical clues to investigate and catch lawbreakers.

Writing Children's Books : A FUN task that allows you to write, illustrate, and publish your own book for young children.

Counted Cross-Stitch: Open to all students interested in doing counted cross-stitch. Everyone completes a simple required project.

Apple Graphics : Learn to make graphic illustrations using the computer.

U.S. and World Puzzles: Learn to do hard puzzles by applying different thinking skills to clues.

Knitting and Crocheting: A variety of needlecraft projects involving knitting, crocheting, counted cross-stitch, or quick points.

Chess: Come and learn chess with a chess master from our community.

Top Gun: Learn about aviation history and military aircraft in the Army, Navy, Air Force, and Marine Corps.

Photography: A basic photography course that will help you take better pictures.

Transportation Models: Start a collection of models — aircraft or automobiles.

Green Thumb: A class to familiarize you with the care and growth of common plants — house and garden.

Drawing: Have you ever wanted to be able to draw some basic designs that looked like you wanted them to look? This class will focus on the basic principles of drawing.

Watercolor: Beginning watercolor makes you sensitive to the delicate shades that are possible.

Sketching and Cartooning: Bring your clever ideas here and let us help you draw sketches and cartoons to make them come to life.

Herpetology : Interested in snakes, lizards, and frogs? Learn how to respect and care for these unique critters.

Trivial Pursuit: This game is enjoyed by all who like to store up a wide variety of facts and amaze your friends with what you know.

Word Power: People that have a great vocabulary have real power in their grasp. They can find words to express just about anything. Come and improve your vocabulary!

History of Rock and Roll: Come and find out more about the music that has influenced today's popular music.

Balderdash: There is a lot of poppycock in everything we do. This activity takes a look at a lot of stuff and nonsense that involves our whole life.

Band: If you're already in band we want you to help us become the best there is. If you're not in band and play an instrument, we need you.

Chorus: Come learn basic vocal production, part singing, and concert-performance techniques.

Technology Student Association: An ongoing activity involving school services and community projects. Come in and check us out. Perhaps you would enjoy what we do.

Future Homemakers of America: A club for boys and girls with the overall goal to help individuals improve personal, family, and community living. You're welcome to see what we do.

Intramural Volleyball : A great game open to all who would like to play. Teams are organized and a tournament format is followed.

Intramural Soccer: The popularity of soccer is sweeping through the country. You can learn about this game and have fun too.

Intramural Basketball: Basketball is a fast-paced game where no one stands around waiting for something to happen. This game demands good teamwork.

Intramural Flag Football: A good team sport that has removed a lot of the danger of contact football. There is a place for everyone on our teams.

Newspaper: For those who like to write, this is a great activity. The regularly published school newspaper gives students a chance to share their talents with the entire school.

School leaders at Daniel Morgan believe their mini-course program is an essential part of the total curriculum. After six years of operation, the activities have evolved to a position that they are integral to everything that goes on in the school. They continue to be very popular with the students. Teachers and parents agree that the experiences are both valuable and important.

SHELBURNE MIDDLE SCHOOL, SHELBURNE, VERMONT

The award for the most creative use of time in scheduling a seven-period day should probably be given to Shelburne Middle School. A 200-minute block of time is scheduled during the morning for academic subjects. During the afternoons there are three 40-minute periods. On Tuesdays and Thursdays, these periods are given over to their interdisciplinary studies program. On Mondays, Wednesdays, and Fridays, Shelburne Middle School devotes it afternoons to elective courses. Each of these programs will be discussed separately because of the different contributions they make to the total exploratory curriculum.

In the interdisciplinary studies all of the students and all the teachers in Grades 5-8 are divided among three different multi-age groups:

The Technology Team is composed of such faculty as mathematics, science, practical arts, living arts (home economics), and certain fifth grade faculty.

The Humanities Team selects its faculty from language arts, social studies, art, music, physical education, and certain fifth grade teachers.

The Communications Team has representatives from language arts, foreign language, keyboarding (typing and computers), mathematics, physical education, and certain fifth grade teachers.

Each group is a multi-age group that meets two afternoons every week for twelve weeks.

Every student has the opportunity to experience each team every year.

These three teams plan around an annual theme. One year the theme was "A Limited Earth." The Technology Team chose to concentrate on natural resources and the options available to earth's inhabitants in regard to the use of energy. The Humanities Team decided to compare life in Vermont with life in China. What similarities are there in the way we live? What are the differences between how we live in Vermont when compared to how they live in China? The Communications Team determined to investigate all the various ways people communicate with each other locally and world-wide. How many different ways can we distribute information around the world?

Students were hesitant to become involved with multi-aged groups. Both older and younger students were very apprehensive about working together. The staff accepted these feelings as a challenge and planned several interesting activities to help students feel more secure in this new arrangement. From the very beginning of interdisciplinary studies teachers reported, however, that there was noticeably less competition and more cooperation among students.

The notion of interdisciplinary studies is consonant with the idea of exploration. Although an in-depth evaluation of its affect on total curriculum has not yet been completed there are many encouraging results noted. The blend of efforts of a relatively large number of staff members has generated an abundance of ideas. Faculty are finding that concepts they are trying to teach in their specialized fields are powerfully reinforced in interdisciplinary studies. The multi-age grouping has improved the relationship between teachers and students. In the course of a year, every student in school gets some exposure to every teacher in the school. The sense of community is greatly enhanced for everyone in Shelburne Middle School. The interdisciplinary studies program helps create a transition school for both students and teachers. For students, these studies help make a smooth transition from self-contained classrooms in the early grades to specialized subjects in the high school. This particular school integrated the teaching of those who were accustomed to self-contained classrooms with those who had specific subject matter interests and education. Teachers who had adapted to teaching in relative isolation found it stimulating to work more closely with others. All teachers found it exhilarating to experiment with different grouping patterns and different styles of teaching.

This concept is still young at Shelburne Middle School, but the results are encouraging. Confidence in trying new things continues to grow. The school enrollment is quite small (about 300 students).

Accompanying interdisciplinary studies is an elective program that is scheduled three afternoons each week. Students select four choices of electives in order of preference. The elective classes meet one, two, or three times each week depending on the specific activity. There is a great deal of flexibility evident in the scheduling of time. The value of exploration to the total curriculum was ranked as very high. The elective program, like interdisciplinary studies, meets for a twelve-weeks session. On this schedule, some teachers teach as many as four different activities during the six periods that electives are offered.

As an example, during 5th period on Tuesday and Wednesday, an art teacher is scheduled for a basic drawing activity in which students explore with the use of pen and ink, pencil, or chalk. On Friday, 5th period, this same teacher teams with another teacher to produce children's art to illustrate writing about holiday customs in the United States that will be shared with children in Russia. During 6th period on Tuesday, this art teacher teams with another teacher in studio and video production to design scenery, props, and graphics. On Friday during 6th period, this teacher has yet a fourth activity entitled "Painting Like the Famous Artists" in which students study the techniques used by some of the great artists. Then they try some of the techniques themselves.

In widely different ways during one twelve-week period all teachers in this school presented a wide array of elective activities, some of which are scheduled for one period of the six and others for as many as three periods every week.

Besides offering chorus and band, some of the other electives offered in this flexible program include the following:

Stocks: Buying and selling on stock market.

World of Theater: A look at different theatrical presentations including comedy and tragedy.

Practical Arts: Exploring unusual processes of making wooden articles.

Living Arts: Food and nutrition, fabric design.

Bookoverdosers: Explore the unknown through reading.

Current Events: Politics in the nation and the world, local events.

Great Books (7th and 8th grades): Book discussions.

Quilting: Learn the art of hand quilting.

Chess: Learn the game — challenge your mind.

Directions Ace (5th and 6th grades): Fun activities to help you follow directions in everyday life.

Video Production: Basic video and audio techniques.

Knitting: Make simple projects, visit a yarn shop. This is a beginning class.

Mind Games: Thinking through problems and using logical thought in games.

Creative Writing: Exploring different styles of writing.

News, Information, Sports: Basic video and audio production practices and techniques.

Gab Session: Talking about your concerns and interests.

Drama: Acting, make-up, and improvisation techniques.

Animal Tracking: Great variety of projects to help you understand the characteristics of different animals.

Urban Geography: Learn all about cities and how they are designed.

Page Power: How to write various types with a special emphasis on letter writing.

Personal Writing: Writings based on personal experience are revised and put into finished form.

Jr. Great Books (5th and 6th grades): Book discussions.

Writing With a Word Processor: Many writing experiences in a computer laboratory. Through telecommunications writings are exchanged with another school.

Performing Arts: Select songs and perform through singing, dancing, and playing musical instruments.

Newsroom: Preparing a school newspaper, interviewing, illustrating, typing, and selling advertisements.

Astronomy I: Study the solar system from its origins to the present.

Computer: Logo program in the computer laboratory.

Math Counts: Practice difficult math problems and prepare for math contests.

Cross-Stitch Embroidery: Basic embroidery completing projects from books or your own design.

Astronomy II: The power of the sun in our solar system.

These activities represent just those offered during one twelve-weeks period. Many others would be offered during other periods of the year.

MARSHALL SIMONDS MIDDLE SCHOOL, BURLINGTON, MASSACHUSETTS

Marshall Simonds Middle School is recognized throughout New England as a "true" middle school. Educators flock to observe the wide array of exemplary programs and educational practices that are in place. The diversified exploratory program features varying time blocks and a unique activity block that has been a feature of this program for more than seventeen years.

At Marshall Simonds Middle School the exploratory program is part of a plan, part of the goals, part of an idea. It is not possible to look at only the exploratory program without looking at some of the broader purposes for the middle school. The school has a philosophy that has been developed for the whole school and its program. It also makes a statement in support of exploratory education without ever saying "exploration."

> *The basic philosophy of the Marshall Simonds Middle School focuses on an educational program that recognizes and provides for the uniqueness of the individual. Each pupil has physical, social, and intellectual characteristics that are different from those of other pupils and that should be considered in providing for his/her educational needs. Through opportunities for independent study and interactions fostered by group endeavors each pupil should discover not only his/her own self worth and potential, but also a sensitivity toward human relationships and respect for the abilities, values, and attitudes of others.*

> *Each student should have an opportunity for achieving maximum growth in self-knowledge, in personal discipline, in citizenship, and in diversified academic experiences. Respect for and trust in the child are basic principles along with the assumption that all children want to learn. If the emphasis is on learning and not on teaching, on each child's thinking process and not on rote skill acquisition, on freedom*

and responsibility rather than conformity and following direction, desired growth will occur. The program should help students to understand the nature of adolescence, its problems, joys, privileges, and responsibilities.

This philosophy supports a strong academic curriculum as well as a full and complete exploratory program.

The exploratory program at Marshall Simonds includes the traditional exploratory courses of music, art, home economics, technology education, foreign language, computer education, and health and physical education. The schedule is built on larger and smaller blocks of time depending on the time requirements of each course. Times vary from forty (40) minutes for music classes, to fifty (50) minutes for art and foreign language, to sixty (60) minutes for physical education and home economics. It is refreshing to see a school schedule with variable times. The time for exploratory offerings provides common planning time for academic teams and vice versa.

One of the strong features of the exploratory curriculum at Marshall Simonds Middle School is the activity block. On Tuesday and Thursday afternoons, for forty minutes, students select from more than seventy (70) mini-courses to enroll in for a period of five weeks. At the end of five weeks they have the option of selecting a new activity or, in many cases, they can continue in the same mini-course. All of the teachers are involved in this program and they have the autonomy to offer any course they feel will be relevant and interesting to middle school students. Students, too, have the autonomy to select any course they would like to experience. They have the opportunity to work with teachers and students from other teams in the school. It is possible to investigate any activity free of anxiety in an atmosphere of respect, cooperation, and fun. Each student is placed in an activity of his choice in a hands-on process. For most students, this block of time allows them to feel confident and successful.

At Marshall Simonds they recognize that young adolescents have wide but fleeting interests. Providing many exploratory activities that introduce students to a variety of topics, skills, and content fields without requiring mastery is developmentally most appropriate. The wide variety of mini-courses or elective units gives students some control over the kinds of learning they will undertake and gives them variety.

It takes a lot of courage to face a community that has always supported an interscholastic sports program and tell them that there really is no place for interscholastic sports in the middle school. Marshall Simonds has installed a strong intramural sports program in which all young adolescents can participate. In addition to the many sports necessary to a full intramural program, there are specialized art classes, computer classes, and a wide variety of crafts that have been found to be very popular.

After seventeen years the exploratory program is rated as very important to the total curriculum. Teachers are in a position to see the value of exploration not only to the students but in their relationships with students. Parents also view this program as very important for their children. They understand the purpose of exploration. Students find the activities very valuable and demonstrate their enthusiasm by getting involved. Exploration at Marshall Simonds Middle School has withstood the test of time.

The impressive list of offerings from which approximately seventy (70) are offered during each five-weeks period is comprised of the following choices:

ACTIVITY BLOCK OFFERINGS

Aviation
Backpacking
Baking and Decorating
Food
Ballet
Band
Basketball
Bike Repair
Block Art
Bread Dough
Bread Making
Bridge
Bulletin Board Preparation
Cake Decorating
Calisthenics
Calculator Games
Calligraphy (Handwriting)
Camping Skills
Christmas Wreaths
Cinematography
Clothing
Coin Collecting
Computers
Conservation
Cooking (Greek, Italian,
Oriental, Vegetarian,
Mexican Copper
Enameling
Copper Tooling
Cosmetology
Creative Arts
Creative Writing
Crewel Embroidery
Cribbage

Crocheting
Current Events
Cycle Repairs
Dancing
Debate
Decoupage
Drama Club
Electricity
Electronics
Embroidery
Enamel Jewelry Making
Fashion
Fashion Design
Figure Drawing
First Aid
Flowers
Folk Dancing
Foreign Dancing
French Cooking
Gem & Mineral Center
Geometric Prisms
Gift Wrapping
Girls Home Mechanics
Golf
Gourmet Cooking
Granny Afghan Squares
Great Books
Guitar Mosaics
Hair & Clothing Fashions
Holiday Decorations
Holiday Gifts and Crafts
Home Repairs
Horticulture
Household Electricity

Household Maintenance
How to Study
Indians of the West
Jewelry Making
Jogging
Kickball
Kites
Knitting
LaCrosse
Lapidary
Law
Leaders Club
Leatherworking
Library Aide
Linoleum Block
Liquid Embroidery
Locks and Safes
Macrame
Magic Glass and Bottle Art
Making Mobiles
Making Stained Glass
Map Making
Math Club
Math Skill Games
Mechanical Drawing
Meteorology
Model and Rocket Building
Model Building
Modeling
Nature Study
Needle Point
Newspaper
Novice Amateur Radio
   Operator

Nurses Club
Oceanography
Oil Painting by Number
One-Act Plays
Oriental Painting
Pantomime
Paper-maché Jewelry
Patchwork Embroidery
Pen Pals
Photography
Physical Fitness
Pickle People
Ping Pong
Poetry
Poster Fun
Pottery
Prose and Poetry
Psychology
Public Speaking and
Debates
Puppetry
Puzzles
Quilting

Rocks and Minerals
Rug Hooking
Science Club
Science Fiction
Scrabble
Sculpting with Nuts and
Bolts
Sculpture
Secret Codes
Shorthand
Sign Language
Silk Screening
Singing for Fun
Slide Rule Use
Soap Sculpture
Speed Reading
Stamps
Stocks and Bonds
Story Telling
Street Hockey
String Art
Student Council
Studio Art Classes

Study Time
Stuffed Animals
Styrofoam Fun
Survival Club
Tap Dancing
Taxidermy
Trampoline
Travel
Travel Tips for Students
Trimnastics
Tropical Fish
Tutoring
Tie Dyeing
Volleyball
Water Colors
Wax Sculpture
Weight Lifting
Wild Plants
Wood Carving
Wood Crafts
Wood Plaques
Yard Clean Up
Yarn Flowers

CARLETON W. WASHBURNE SCHOOL, WINNETKA, ILLINOIS

Carleton W. Washburne School has a program of exploratory courses required of all students in the sixth and seventh grades. Eighth grade students have the option of choosing from several elective course offerings. The key phrase for describing this exploratory program would be "planned structure." Their schedule is nine 40-minute periods with a short (5 minutes) advisory time at the beginning of the day and a longer (24 minutes) advisory period after 9th period.

Sixth grade students are assigned to two-teacher teams for their core academic program. Two periods of exploratory classes are assigned every day to sixth grade students. These two classes are scheduled for 6 or 12 weeks so that, at the end of the sixth grade, each student will have experienced nine different offerings. The only exceptions are students who play in either the band or the orchestra. These students may select one of the exploratory courses each trimester. Band and orchestra meet during one period daily.

The exploratory offerings include:

Art - Students work with flat surfaces and with solid objects using a variety of materials. They are expected to demonstrate some initiative and resourcefulness in this course.

General Music - This course is a general music seven week course in discipline-based instruction with balanced training in criticism, history, aesthetics and performance. Students are familiar with styles and historical context of works.

Home Economics - Students cooperate in three complete kitchens to prepare a variety of foods. They learn good cooking skills and hygiene as well as good nutritional habits.

Industrial Arts - Students organize their work, show pride in their work, practice safety, and demonstrate good use and care of equipment. The main objective is to develop basic skills, some of which may serve as a basis for further learning at the eighth grade level.

French/Spanish - Each student has the option of selecting French and/or Spanish as an exploratory activity. During the seventh and eighth grades, students may continue with foreign language one period each day. Those completing two years in foreign language receive one credit in foreign language at the high school level. At the seventh grade level, the Spanish program is enhanced by a visit to Little Village, an Hispanic inner-city barrio, where students tour a tortillema, make purchases in Spanish, and lunch at a Mexican restaurant.

Keyboard Skills - Students learn to use correct keyboard techniques to develop accuracy and speed. Students develop word processing skills: how to create, save and reload files, edit and format text.

Modern Communication - This course consists of writing, speaking, and production. Students outline and speak from notes making eye contact with the audience, using good diction and volume, displaying emotion. Their completed speeches may be used to introduce, demonstrate, inform, convince, announce, or entertain. In the television section of this exploratory course, students complete a first television production, a graphic assignment, and a final project.

Washburne feels that the exploratory program is an essential component of a well balanced curriculum. All students in sixth grade participate actively in a wide range of carefully chosen and planned practical and fine arts courses.

Seventh and eighth grade students are placed on teams, each consisting of two sections (40-45 students) at the seventh grade level and about the same number of students at the eighth grade level. Five staff members are assigned to each team. One math, science, and social studies teacher each teach two sections of students at each grade level; two English teachers are assigned to each team — one teacher working a double period at the seventh grade level and one at the eighth grade level.

Three 12-week exploratories are required of each seventh grade student: computers, dramatics, general music.

During the second exploratory period seventh graders, in conjunction with their parents, may choose to select French or Spanish or one trimester each of art, journalism, and global awareness.

Resource assistance is available to those students who may benefit from additional help and support in any of the academic areas.

Descriptions of the three exploratory courses required for seventh grade students and the foreign language option are.

Computers - During this trimester students become literate in the use of basic terms and commands used with computers. They gain ability to organize working programs and show initiative in solving computer problems.

Drama - Following instruction and experience in pantomime and creative dramatics, students move to Theater Production. Classwork includes training in all production skills as well as in acting and performance skills.

General Music - An extension of general music in the sixth grade in which they attended to basic rhythm, melody, and harmony in music. In addition, they are introduced to musical symbols including dynamics, tempo markings, and time signatures. They become acquainted with the various musical media: symphony, band, chorus, ballet, oratorio, opera, and musical theater.

French/Spanish is an outgrowth of the exploratory in foreign language at the sixth grade level. Those who successfully complete French I or Spanish I at the seventh grade level are enrolled in French II or Spanish II at the eighth grade.

Those who complete two years of foreign language at Washburne receive one year of high school credit. In Spanish, students study muralism and visit the murals of Pilsen, another inner-city barrio. They also correspond with students from an inner-city Hispanic school and exchange visits with them. The idea is to use Spanish beyond the classroom and foster cross-cultural understanding.

Those students who prefer to delay their language until high school take one trimester of:

Art - Students participate in both individual and group art activities, with emphasis on process rather than product. Creativity and problem-solving skills are developed through a variety of projects. Students will also gain an understanding of the elements of design and the color wheel.

Journalism - Students will write and edit their own work and collect literary pieces from the members of the Washburne community in order to publish the Washburne Literary Journal. Desktop publishing skills (layout, text, graphics) is taught along with journalism skills. Students use their creativity to design and publish the journal.

Global Awareness - The cultural diversity of metropolitan Chicago is utilized so that students participate in a variety of experiences, activities, and projects that expand their awareness of world cultures.

Eighth graders are in a five-teacher team for English (2 periods), social studies, math, and science classes. Students have one period daily of physical education and two electives, chosen from the following: art, musical play production, debate, drama, homemaking, industrial arts, modern communication, foreign language, advanced chorus, computers, and journalism/yearbook. band/orchestra for seventh and eighth graders is offered early in the morning before school.

Individual student needs are served through the following programs: Developmental Learning Services, Learning Disabilities Program, Reading Improvement, Social Work, and Speech Therapy.

At the eighth grade level, Washburne has an elective program which is still exploratory in nature. Each course is scheduled for one trimester and the students, along with their parents, have the opportunity to make their own choices. The electives include the following:

Art	Advanced Chorus
Debate	Drama
French or Spanish	Homemaking
Industrial Arts	Journalism/Yearbook
Junior Office Assistant	Keyboard/Computer
Modern Communications	Musical Play Productions

At Washburne, educators have built a three year structure for their exploratory program. It is rich and varied throughout grades 6-8 with an air of permanence about the program. They have experienced wide success with these exploratory offerings and electives. A "Satisfactory" and "Needs Improvement" system of grading courses is used in the exploratory areas in the 6th and 7th grades along with a very detailed evaluation for every element which assesses skills, knowledge, attitudes, and effort.

CHAPTER EIGHT

Evaluating the Exploratory Program

E valuating an exploratory program involves using different ap--
proaches and techniques than those used in evaluating other
components of the curriculum. Middle grade students will be
evaluating every part of the exploratory program as they make personal
decisions about the areas they'd like to study. It is just as important for students
to identify areas in which they have low interest and little capability as it is to find
areas in which they excel and have high interest. From this standpoint evaluation
poses no threat to students. There are no standardized tests for measuring either
achievement or interest in exploratory areas, and there shouldn't be. Such
evaluation also provides feedback to teachers, parents, and community, helping
them think more clearly about the broad goals of education. The feedback on the
exploratory program must somehow tie into everything valued by the school. It
is not enough to evaluate a part of the curriculum that might be labeled
exploratory. An evaluation of the exploratory curriculum should be in the
context of the total program. Because the exploratory curriculum is continually
changing, formative evaluation takes on added significance. Evaluation approaches must be sensitive to the changes that take place in the objectives, the
participants, and even the teachers of these experiences.

Student Self-evaluation

Student self-evaluation is the most important aspect of the entire exploratory
evaluation effort. What happens within the middle grade learner is basic. The
program ought to be helping the students develop valid and healthy images of
themselves. It must also enrich their perceptions of the world around them,
expand their vision of opportunities and choices open to them, and appraise
realistically their residual weaknesses and limitations. Self-evaluation can lead
students to gain enthusiasm for various learning activities and a better conception of themselves, their values, and ultimate goals.

The traditional ABC grading system is a procedure that everyone knows but no one really understands, and few recognize its serious limitations. Kelley (1952) said it is a shame that in a culture with a language as rich as ours we still try to describe a person with a single letter! Psychologists and psychiatrists have pointed out the undesirable effects that grades cause on the mental health of students. These arguments against traditional grades have not gone unnoticed, but acceptable alternatives seem to remain beyond our reach.

There are several reasons that efforts to change grading systems have led to very little action. No consensus on any substitute for grades has emerged. Those who are successful in receiving good grades have a genuine interest in continuing them — and so do their parents. College entrance requirements perpetuate grades because good grades in public school predict good grades in college. Teachers realize that they are not omniscient, and they want to be as objective and fair about grades as is possible, so they accept grades as a difficult but inevitable part of teaching.

Self-evaluation is central to student growth and its importance must be more widely recognized. Students are not accidental results of what happens to them. They are choice-makers who hope, care, and strive to be effective in life. They are developing a concept of adequacy for themselves, seeking to become valuable and worthy to others. They want to be a part of the world in a way that really counts and to be independent and autonomous. This concept of adequacy implies evaluation and self-evaluation that works for each individual student.

It would be well if all evaluation procedures in our schools could be revolutionized. While such changes will evolve slowly, it is possible to start a revolution with the evaluation procedures used in the exploratory courses. Teachers can make these activities so rich in experiences that exploring, choice-making, and evaluating will be intrinsically satisfying and no one is concerned about grades. The teachers must form ideas about what goal each student is pursuing and plan ways that each student can find success.

The first step in self-evaluation involves having all learners establish their own purposes. Students need to realize they are not necessarily expected to do what the teacher has in mind for them but rather what they have in mind for themselves. Students then set the criteria they will accept as evidence that they are in pursuit of their goal and have achieved success in that activity. The teacher can help the students devise for themselves ways of achieving their goals and recognizing their accomplishments.

Self-evaluation leads students to becoming self-directed. It takes courage on the part of teachers to allow self-direction to happen. Teachers typically feel that if they do not require certain standards and push students to achieve them students would do little. Students have spent years doing "school" tasks that someone else has required of them. When they are given the chance to establish learnings meaningful to them, to work at levels where they feel confident, and to set their own evaluation criteria it will take time for them to accept and use this new responsibility and overcome their prior conditioning.

The teacher's role in encouraging self-direction will require use of some subtle ways. Instead of directing students with statements such as "Do this" or "Why don't you try this?", they will ask questions such as "What do you think you should do now?" At first students will give responses they think teachers want to hear. Teachers must question these responses to make them the student's responses. In answer to questions like "What is right?" or "What should I do?" or "What do I do next?" the teacher should respond with "What do you think?" or "What is most important to you?" Students must not lose favor with the teacher if they fail to accomplish their own goals in an exploratory class. Mastery is not the purpose of exploratory activities. It is inherently disappointing for students to fail in fulfilling their own objectives, but they can accept that disappointment if the teacher does not also penalize them — by low grades, words, or more assignments to make up for their failures. When learning is life-related and interest-related to the student and the teacher alike, self-direction and self-evaluation take place naturally.

Teachers should keep records of the conferences they hold with individual students. These records will give direction for the exploratory instruction. Individual conferences do not need to be long but they are valuable for both the students and the teacher. They make it possible for the teacher to know more about the individual goals of each student. They are also beneficial because the student sees that the teacher is interested in each individual student.

Corey (1944) related the apocryphal story he entitled "The Poor Scholar's Soliloquy" in which a middle grade learner is faced with a curriculum that is not relevant. In social studies he had difficulty memorizing thirty Presidents and then thirty Vice-Presidents. When he repeated the grade he had a teacher who wasn't interested in Presidents but had them memorizing great inventors. He had trouble writing about "What a Daffodil Thinks of Spring" but had no trouble writing 17 letters to farmers about how well their livestock sold in the Chicago stockyards. He didn't even do well in industrial arts because he had to build something out of wood that didn't interest him instead of making an endgate for his uncle's trailer that did interest him. He was a bright young man who was caught in the school trap doing "school" things that really didn't interest him.

A dynamic self-evaluation is the most important kind of student evaluation in middle grades not just for exploratory activities but for all subjects in the curriculum. Certainly it should be used throughout the exploratory program. Middle grade students need this empowerment to help them take the responsibility for their own learning.

Program Evaluation

Having a functioning student self-evaluation model will not relieve the school of responsibility for developing a program evaluation model for the exploratory program. There are several models that would seem appropriate for this task. In a larger school system having well developed exploratory programs in some schools and less well developed programs in others, there would be the possibility to set up comparison groups to evaluate several hypotheses related to the impact of the middle grade exploratory program. It could be hypothesized that middle grade students in schools with exploratory programs will have more favorable attitudes toward school than pupils in schools without exploratory programs. This hypothesis could be tested with a questionnaire. It could also be tested unobtrusively by comparing the attendance records of both schools. Over several years, the drop out rates could be compared as another measure of favorable attitude toward schools.

Teachers in middle level schools with exploratory programs are likely to experience a higher degree of professional fulfillment and satisfaction than teachers in schools without an exploratory program. This hypothesis could be checked. Other hypotheses would say that achievement scores are enhanced in middle level schools in which an exploratory program is in place, that creativity will be higher among middle level students who are more involved in exploratory activities, and that parents of middle level students who are experiencing a good exploratory program will hold more positive attitudes toward objectives and procedures of their schools when compared to schools with a less effective exploratory program. The hypothesis model is one way to evaluate the program from the outside. The results could be used to justify beginning an exploratory program in schools where very little effort has gone into an exploratory program.

There are models of evaluation that can be conducted within a school. One model would be the responsive model, sometimes called the democratic pluralism model. It is oriented more toward program activities than to program intents. Evaluators use issues in the evaluation process rather than specific hypotheses or objectives. They determine what they wish to evaluate and set the criteria they should be able to observe. Observations are conducted and the data are returned to evaluators for processing. The evaluators process the information and present a report to patrons of the school, to teachers in the school, or to the school system. Evaluators do not judge the report. They offer neither criticisms nor endorsements.

Another technique for evaluating a program would be through a shadow study. It views the program through the eyes of the student rather than the teacher. The shadow study generates qualitative or naturalistic research data that are very effective for staff development of teachers because they give a holistic picture of the day of a student. In the shadow study an observer randomly selects a student and follows that student throughout the day. The observer makes notes on what the student is doing at five-minute intervals and compiles the information as a report. These qualitative data give a wealth of surprising information that gives a view of the school program that is not otherwise obtained.

The goal free model works very well in evaluating an exploratory program. Lipsitz (1984) conducted a substantive goal free evaluation of four schools which presented thorough description of what went on in each school to qualify it as a successful school. A very important part of each school was its emphasis on exploratory activities. This model is used primarily as a summative evaluation. It is imperative that unbiased observers well acquainted with middle level students and schools be used. The criteria for use in the observations must be fully developed and completely accepted. For its use in an exploratory program the criteria could include the scope of exploratory offerings, attitudes of the students, attitudes of the teachers, attitudes of school leaders, attitudes of parents, interests of the students, interests of the teachers, or the self-evaluation taking place. The goal free model is a comprehensive evaluation of the entire school that includes an in-depth view of the school community, interviews of the entire staff to gain a historical perspective of the program as well as attitudes toward the exploratory program, observations in the classroom for several days of schooling, and a complete review of all test data. Although the report that is generated by a goal free evaluation contains some quantitative data it is generally a qualitative evaluation. A recent National Middle School Association publication, *How To Evaluate Your Middle School* (Schurr, 1992), provides excellent directions for conducting an informal evaluation and includes sample survey instruments.

REFERENCES

Adler, M. & McCarroll, J. (1981). *Making music fun.* West Nyack, NY. Parker Publishing Company.

Alexander, W.M. (1989). Exploration — The heart of the middle school. In M.F. Compton & H.C. Hawn (Eds.), *Planning curriculum in the middle school.* Athens, GA: Georgia Center for Continuing Education.

Alexander, W.M. & George, P.S. (1981). *The exemplary middle school.* New York: Holt, Rinehart & Winston.

Alexander, W.M. & McEwin, C.K. (1989). *Schools in the middle: Status & progress.* Columbus, OH: National Middle School Association.

Alexander, W.M., Williams, E.L., Compton, M., Hines, V.A., Prescott, D. & Kealy, R. (1969). *The emergent middle school.* (2nd ed.). New York: Holt, Rinehart & Winston.

Anti-Defamation League of B'Nai B'Rith. (1982). Extremist groups in the United States. New York: B'Nai B'Rith.

Arhar, J.M. (1992). Interdisciplinary teaming and the social bonding of middle level students. In J.L. Irvin (Ed.), *Transforming middle level education.* Boston: Allyn & Bacon, pp. 139-161.

Artman, J. (1980). *Slanguage.* Carthage, IL: Good Apple, Inc.

Bach, J.S. (1988). *Civil liberties: Opposing viewpoints.* St. Paul, MN: Greenhaven Press.

Barnette, H.H. (1972). The anatomy of extremism. In E.S. West (Ed.), *Extremism, left & right.* Grand Rapids, MI: W.B. Eerdmans Publishing Company.

Batesky, J. (1991). Middle school physical education curriculum: Exposure or indepth instruction. *Middle School Journal, 22,* 7-11.

Beane, J.A. (1990). *A middle school curriculum: From rhetoric to reality.* Columbus, OH: National Middle School Association.

Bell, N. (1983). *Only human: Why we are the way we are.* Covelo, CA: Yolla Bolly Press.

Bergmann, S. (1991). Exploratory programs in the middle level school: A responsive idea. In J.L. Irvin (Ed.), *Transforming middle level education.* Boston: Allyn & Bacon.

Bodanis, D. (1986). *The secret house.* New York: Simon & Schuster.

Bondi, J. (1972). *Developing middle schools: A guidebook.* New York: MSS Information Corporation.

Bosserman, P. (1989). The USA: Modern times and the new solidarity. In A. Olszewska and K. Roberts (Eds.), *Leisure and life style.* London: Sage Publications.

Bouchier, D. (1987). *Radical citizenship.* New York: Schocken Books.

Brazee, E.N. (1987). Exploration in the "regular" curriculum. In E.N. Brazee (Ed.), *Exploratory curriculum at the middle level.* Rowley, MA: New England League of Middle Schools.

Bright, G. & Wheeler, M. (1981). Fair games — unfair games. In Shulte, A. & Smart, J. (Eds.), *Teaching statistics and probability.* Reston, VA: National Council of Teachers of Mathematics.

Burns, M. (1978). *Good for me! All about food in 32 bites.* Boston: Little Brown and Company.

California State Department of Education (1987) *Caught in the middle.* Sacramento, CA: State Department of Education.

Capelluti, J. & Brazee, E.N. (1992). Middle School Curriculum: Making sense. *Middle School Journal, 23,* 11-15.

Carin, A.A. & Sund, R.B. (1989). *Guided discovery activities for elementary school science.* Columbus, OH: Merrill Publishing Co.

Carnegie Council on Adolescent Development's Task Force on Education of Young Adolescents. (1989). *Turning points: Preparing American youth for the 21st century.* Washington, DC: Carnegie Council on Adolescent Development.

Carper, C.E. (1991). The Cardigan experience — An eighth grade integrated curriculum. *Middle School Journal, 23,* 36-40.

Chandler, G.L., Hamilton, M., & Ralph, B. (1991). The place of outdoor challenge experiences in the middle school. *Middle School Journal, 22,* 12-16.

Columbia University. (1989). *The concise Columbia encyclopedia.* New York: Columbia University Press.

Commission on Reorganization of Secondary Education of the National Education Association. (1918). *Cardinal principles of secondary education.* Washington, DC: Department of the Interior, Bureau of Education.

Compton, M.F. (1982). Leisure activities selected by middle school students. Paper presented at the annual meeting of the Georgia Educational Research Association, Atlanta, GA, November 19, 1982.

Compton, M.F. (1983). Middle school curriculum: A new approach. *Bulletin of the National Association of Secondary School Principals, 67,* 39-44.

Compton, M.F. (1984). Balance in the middle school curriculum. In J.H. Lounsbury (Ed.), *Perspectives in middle school education.* Columbus, OH: National Middle School Association.

Compton, M.F. & Skelton, J.R. (1982). A study of selected adolescent problems as presented in contemporary realistic fiction for middle school students. *Adolescence, 17,* 637-645.

Conant, J.B. (1960). *Education in the junior high school years: A memorandum to school boards.* Princeton, NJ: Educational Testing Service.

Connecticut Education Association, Council on Interracial Books for Children and National Education Association. (1981). *Violence, the Ku Klux Klan, and the struggle for equality.* New York: Council on Interracial Books for Children (CIBC) Resource Center.

Connelly, F.M. & Ben-Peretz, M. (1980). Teachers' roles in the using and doing of research and curriculum development. *Journal of Curriculum Studies, 12,* 95-107.

Connelly, F.M. & Clandinin, D.J. (1988). *Teachers as curriculum planners: Narratives of Experience.* New York: Teachers' College Press.

Cooper, K.H. (1968). *Civil liberties: Opposing viewpoints.* St. Paul, MN: Greenhaven Press.

Corey, P. (1944). The poor scholar's soliloquy. In B.R. Gearhart & M.W. Weishahn, *The handicapped student in the regular classroom.* St. Louis, MO: The C.V. Mosby Company.

Council on Middle Level Education (1989). *Middle level education's responsibility for intellectual development.* Reston, VA: National Association of Secondary School Principals.

Cremin, L.A. (1961). *The transformation of the school.* New York: Alfred A. Knopf.

Cross, G. (1990). *A social history of leisure since 1600.* State College, PA: Venture Press.

Davies, M.A. (1992). Are interdisciplinary units worthwhile? Ask students. In J.H. Lounsbury (Ed.), *Connecting the curriculum through interdisciplinary instruction.* Columbus, OH: National Middle School Association.

Davis, C.L. (1987). Developmental characteristics as rationale. In E.N. Brazee (Ed.), *Exploratory curriculum at the middle level.* Rowley, MA: New England League of Middle Schools.

Deller, D.K. & Wright, J.E. (1977). An associate faculty program incorporates community resources. *Middle School Journal, 8,* 11.

Denisoff, R.S. (1974). *The sociology of dissent.* New York: Harcourt Brace Jovanovich.

Division of Curriculum Services, Georgia Department of Education. (1982). *Middle grades physical education, grades 5-8*. Atlanta, GA: Georgia Department of Education.

Doda, N. (1981). Exploration: The middle school music. *Teacher to teacher*. Fairborn, OH: National Middle School Association.

Donovan, M. (1985). *Research challenges: Through the use of the atlas, the almanac, and other world resources*. Carthage, IL: Good Apple.

Eichhorn, D.H. (1972). The emerging adolescent school of the future — now. In J.G. Saylor (Ed.), *The school of the future — now*. Washington, DC: Association for Supervision and Curriculum Development.

Eichhorn, D.H. (1966). *The middle school*. Reissued 1987, Columbus, OH: National Middle School Association.

Eichhorn, D.H. (1980). The school. In M. Johnson, Jr. (Ed.), *Toward adolescence: The middle school years: Seventy-ninth yearbook of the National Society for the Study of Education,* Part I. (pp. 56-73). Chicago, IL: University of Chicago Press.

Elkind, D. (1984). *All grown up and no place to go: Teenagers in crisis*. Reading, PA: Addison-Wesley.

Epstein, J.L. & Mac Iver D.J. (1990). *Education in the middle grades*. Columbus, OH: National Middle School Association.

Erb, T.O. & Kilmer, P. (1981). To boost self concepts — open up your activities. *Middle School Journal, 12*, 7, 21-22.

Erb. T.O. & Doda, N. (1989). *Team organization: Promise — practices and possibilities*. Washington, DC: National Education Association.

Faircloth, C.V. (1990). An investigation of attitudes of teachers of exploratory courses toward the planning and utilization of curricula in middle school exploratory programs. Unpublished doctoral dissertation, University of Georgia.

Fallon, D. (1980). *The art of disco dancing*. Reston, VA: National Dance Association.

Feldman, D. (1989). *Who put the butter in butterfly?* New York: Harper & Row.

Forte, I., Frank, M. & MacKenzie, J. (1973). *Kid stuff*. Nashville, TN: Incentive Publications.

Foster, C. & Thompson, L. (1987). Practical considerations and models. In E.N. Brazee (Ed.), *Exploratory curriculum at the middle level*. Rowley, MA: New England League of Middle Schools.

Frisch, R.E. (1974). Critical weight at menarche, initiation of the adolescent growth spurt, and control of puberty. In M.M. Grumbach, G.D. Grave, & F.E. Mayer (Eds.), *The control of the onset of puberty*. New York: John Wiley & Sons.

Gabel, C. (1985). Exploratory activities — Adapting to the 80s. *Middle School Journal, 17,* 22-23.

Gardner, H. (1983). *Frames of mind: The theory of multiple intelligences.* New York: Basic Books.

Gentile, L.M. (1980). *Using sports and physical education to strengthen reading skills.* Newark, DE: International Reading Association.

Gentry, D.L. & Hayes, R.L. (1991). Guidelines for athletic programs in the middle school. *Middle School Journal, 22,* 4-6.

George, P.S. (1983). Confessions of a consultant. Middle school mistakes we made. *Middle School Journal, 14,* 3-6.

George, P.S. (1986). Middle school: Separate & unique. In M.F. Compton & H.C. Hawn (Eds.), *Middle school.* Athens, GA: Center for Continuing Education.

George, P.S. & Lawrence, G. (1982). *Handbook for middle school teaching.* Glenview, IL: Scott, Foresman & Company.

Gerth, E., Bauer, J., Manley, R., Chaney, T. & Smith, J.T. (1977). An exploratory approach to fine and practical arts. *Middle School Journal, 8,* 14-15.

Glatthorn, A.A. (1987). *Curriculum leadership.* Glenview, IL: Scott, Foresman & Company.

Glickman, C. (1990). *Supervision of instruction: A developmental approach.* (2nd Ed.). Boston, MA: Allyn & Bacon.

Goodlad, J. (1984). *A place called school: Prospects for the future.* New York: McGraw-Hill.

Governor's Conference (1991). *America 2000.* Washington, DC: U.S. Printing Office.

Grambs, J.D. & Waetjen, W.B. (1975). *Sex: Does it make a difference?* North Scituate, MA: Duxbury Press.

Gray, T. (1984). Comparative evaluation of elementary school foreign language programs: Final report. In Brandt, R. (Ed.), *Content of the curriculum.* Washington, DC: Association for Supervision and Curriculum Development, p. 103.

Gruhn, W.T. & Douglass, H.R. (1971). *Modern junior high school.* New York: Roland Press.

Halas, J.M. (1991). Evaluating student feedback in physical education: An open approach. *Middle School Journal, 22,* 17-19.

Hall, G.E. & Hord, S.M. (1987). *Change in schools: Facilitating the process.* New York: SUNY Press.

Heneveld, W. (1987). Integrating curriculum development and teacher development in schools. *Prospects, 17,* 98-105.

Hirsch, E.D., Jr., Kett, J.F., & Trefil, J. (1988). *Dictionary of cultural literacy.* Boston, MA: Houghton Mifflin.

Honig, B. (1987). Foreword. In *English-language arts framework.* Sacramento, CA: California State Department of Education.

Hubbard, G. & Rouse, M. (1977). *Art: Discovering and creating.* Westchester, IL: Benefic Press.

Hunter, E. (1988). Adolescent suicide: Cries for help. *Bulletin of the National Association of Secondary School Principals, 72,* 92-94.

Ibrahim, H. (1991). *Leisure and society: A comparative approach.* Dubuque, IA: Wm. C. Brown.

Jackson, C. (1985). *Color me beautiful.* New York: Ballentine.

Jellstrom, B.K. (1976). *Map & compass — The orienteering handbook.* New York: Scribners.

Jewett, A.E. & Bain, L.L. (1985). *The curriculum process in physical education.* Dubuque, IA: Wm C. Brown.

Kelley, E. (1947). *Education for what is real.* New York: Harper and Brothers.

Kercher, L. (1983). A business simulation as an exploratory course. *Middle School Journal, 14,* 16-17.

Kimpston, R.D. & Rogers, K.B. (1988). Predispositions, participatory roles and perceptions of teachers, principals, and community leaders in a collaborative curriculum planning process. *Journal of Curriculum Studies, 20,* 351-367.

Kindred, L.W., Wolotkiewicz, R.J., Mickelson, J.M., Coplein, L.E., and Dyson, E. (1976). *The middle school curriculum: A practitioner's handbook.* Boston: Allyn & Bacon.

Kubler-Ross, E. (1987). *Aids: The ultimate challenge.* New York: Macmillan Publishing Co.

Lambert, L.T. & Trimble, R.T. (1987). *The basic stuff in action for grades 4-8.* Reston, VA: American Alliance for Health, Physical Education, Recreation, and Dance.

Lapointe, A.E., Mead, N.A., & Phillips, G.W. (1989). *A world of differences: An international assessment of mathematics and science.* Princeton, NJ: Educational Testing Service.

Lerner, R.M. & Spanier, G.B. (1980). *Adolescent development: A life-span perspective*. New York: McGraw-Hill.

Lieberman, A. (1982). Practice makes policy: The tensions of school improvement. In A. Lieberman & M.W. McLaughlin (Eds.), *Policy making in education: Eighty-first yearbook of the National Society for the Study of Education*. pp. 249-269. Chicago, IL: University of Chicago Press.

Lipsitz, J.S. (1983). *Successful schools for young adolescents*. New Brunswick, NJ: Transaction Books.

Lounsbury, J.H. (1991). A fresh start for the middle school curriculum. *Middle School Journal, 23*, 29-35.

Lounsbury, J.H. (1991). *As I see it*. Columbus, OH: National Middle School Association.

Lounsbury, J.H. (Ed.) (1992). *Connecting the curriculum through interdisciplinary instruction*. Columbus, OH: National Middle School Association.

Lounsbury, J.H. & Vars, G.F. (1978). *A curriculum for the middle school years*. New York: Harper & Row.

Macaulay, D. (1988). *The way things work*. Boston: Houghton Mifflin.

Marquis, D. (1930). *Archy and Mehitabel*. New York: Doubleday.

McDonough, L. (1991). Middle level curriculum: The search for self and social meaning. *Middle School Journal, 23*, 29-35.

McEwin, C.K. & Alexander, W.M. (1990). *Middle level programs and practices in elementary schools*. Columbus, OH: National Middle School Association.

Merenbloom, E.Y. (1988). *Developing effective middle schools through faculty participation*. 2nd Ed. Columbus, OH: National Middle School Association.

Messick, R.G. & Reynolds, K.E. (1992). *Middle level curriculum in action*. White Plains, NY: Longman Publishing Company.

Met, M. (1988). Tomorrow's emphasis in foreign language: Proficiency. In Brandt, R. (Ed.), *Content of the curriculum*. Washington, DC: Association for Supervision and Curriculum Development.

Moeller, T.E. & Valentine, J.W. (1981). Middle schools for the eighties. *Middle School Journal, 12*, 26-30.

Montagu, A. (1970). *The natural superiority of women*. New York: Collier-Macmillan.

Moss, T.C. (1969). *Middle school*. Boston: Houghton Mifflin.

Mundy, J. & Odum, L. (1979). *Leisure education*. New York: John Wiley & Sons.

Naisbitt, J. (1982). *Megatrends*. New York: Warner Books.

Nature Conservancy. (1990). Put your concern to work. *The Nature Conservancy Magazine*, *40*, 12+.

Neulinger, J. *The psychology of leisure*. Springfield, IL: Charles C. Thomas.

Newspaper Enterprise Association. (1991). *The world almanac and book of facts*. New York: United Media Enterprises.

Ott, J.N. (1976). *Health and light*. New York: Pocket Books.

Phelps, J.D. (1987). Exploring the workplace: Middle school career education programs. In E.N. Brazee (Ed.). *Exploratory curriculum at the middle level*. Rowley, MA: New England League of Middle Schools.

Piaget, J. & Inhelder, B. (1958). *Growth of logical thinking from childhood to adolescence*. New York: Basic Books.

Poole, M.G. & O'Keafor, K.R. (1989). The effects of teacher efficacy and interactions among educators on curriculum implementation. *Journal of Curriculum and Supervision*, *2*, 146-161.

Rheingold, H. (1991). *Virtual reality: Exploring the brave new technologies*. New York: Summit Books.

Riegle, J.D. (1971). A study of middle school programs to determine the current level of implementation of eighteen basic middle school principles. Unpublished doctoral dissertation, University of Michigan.

Robinson, G.E. (1975). *Summary of research on middle schools*. Arlington, VA: Educational Research Service, Inc.

Romano, L.G. & Timmers, N. (1978). Middle school athletics — intramurals or interscholastic? *Middle School Journal*, *9*, 3, 16.

Rottier, J. & Whooley, J. (1986). Middle grades educational practices survey. *Middle School Journal*, *17*, 22-24.

Sale, L.L. (1979). *Introduction to middle school teaching*. Columbus, OH: Charles E. Merrill.

Schneider, G.T. (1986). Exploratory programs and educational reform. *Middle School Journal*, *17*, 3, 23.

Schurr, S. (1992). *How to evaluate your middle school*. Columbus, OH: National Middle School Association.

Scudder, C.W. (1972). Psychological dimentions of extremism. In E.S. West (Ed.), *Extremeism Left and Right.* Grand Rapids, MI: Eerdmans Publishing Co.

Shippert, F. (1981). Academic gaming in the middle school. *Middle School Journal, 12,* 13-15.

Snow, M.H. (1989). Embryonic growth and the manipulation of fetal size. In J.M. Tanner & M.A. Preece (Eds.), *The physiology of human growth.* Cambridge: Cambridge University Press.

Spencer, C. (1987). What the literature says about exploratory programs. In E.N. Brazee (Ed.), *Exploratory curriculum for the middle level.* Rowley, MA: New England League of Middle Schools.

Springer, M. (1992). in J.H. Lounsbury, (Ed.), *Connecting the curriculum through interdisciplinary instruction.* Columbus, OH: National Middle School Association.

Steffans, P. (1991). Exploration — The final Frontier. *Middle School Journal, 22,* 30-33.

Steffens, J.B. & Carr, J.F. (1983). *Mystery and suspense: Skill-oriented language arts activities.* Santa Barbara, CA: The Learning Works.

Swift, H. (1983). Peer helping: A successful exploratory course. *Middle School Journal, 14,* 20-21.

Tanner, J.M. (1978). *Foetus into man: Physical growth from conception to maturity.* London: Open Books Publishing, Ltd.

Tanner, J.M. (1962). *Growth at adolescence.* London: Blackwell Scientific Publications.

Thornburg, H.D. (1980). Can the middle school adapt to the needs of its students? *The emerging adolescent: Characteristics and educational implications.* Columbus, OH: National Middle School Association.

Thornburg, H.D. (1983). Is early adolescence really a stage of development? *Theory Into Practice, 22,* 79-84.

Tinnappei, H. (1963). On divisibility rules. In J.H. Hlavaty (Ed.), *Enrichment mathematics for the grades.* Twenty-seventh Yearbook, Reston, VA: National Council of Teachers of Mathematics.

Toepfer, C.F. (1980). Brain growth periodization data: Some suggestions for reorganizing middle grades education. *High School Journal, 63,* 224-226.

Toepfer, C.F. (1980). Brain growth periodization in your adolescents: Some educational implications. ERIC. (ED 187755), April.

Toepfer, C.F. (1992). Curriculum for identity. *Middle School Journal, 23,* 3-10.

Toepfer, C.F. (1982). Junior high and middle school education. In J.E. Mitzel, J.H. Best & W. Rabinowitz (Eds.), *Encyclopedia of Educational Research: Vol. 1*, (pp. 989-1000). New York: Macmillan Publishing Company.

Trump, J.L. & Baynham, D. (1961). *Focus on change.* Skokie, IL: Rand McNally and Company.

Van Til, W., Vars, G.F. & Lounsbury, J.H. (1967). *Modern education for the junior high school years.* 2nd Ed. Indianapolis, IN: Bobbs-Merrill.

Vars, G.F. (1987). *Interdisciplinary teaching in the middle grades.* Columbus, OH: National Middle School Association.

Vars, G.F. (1973). Guidelines for junior high and middle school education. In L.G. Romano, N.P. Georgiady & J.E. Heald (Eds.), *The middle school: Selected readings on an emerging school program.* Chicago: Nelson-Hall Company.

Waddell, H.C. (1972). Common features of extremists' ugly faces. In E.S. West (Ed.), *Extremism left and right.* Grand Rapids, MI: Eerdmans Publishing Company.

Waltz, T.E. (1976). Exploratory teaming: An interdisciplinary approach to the fine and practical arts. *Middle School Journal*, 7, 18-19.

Wigginton, E. (1972). *The foxfire book: Hog dressing; log cabin building; mountain crafts and foods; snake lore; hunting tales; faith healing; moonshining; and other affairs of plain living.* Garden City, NY: Doubleday.

Wiles, J. & Bondi, J. (1981). *The essential middle school.* Columbus, OH: Charles E. Merrill.

Young, J.H. & Small, J.L. (1988). Teachers' motivations for participating in curriculum development committees. *The Alberta Journal of Educational Research*, *34*, 42-56.